★ The Way to U.S. ★
CITIZENSHIP

Margaret W. Hirschy
Patricia L. Hirschy

New, Revised Edition

Dominie Press, Inc.

Publisher: Raymond Yuen
Executive Editor: Carlos A. Byfield
Copy Editor: Becky Colgan
Designer: Jana Whitney
Cover Designer: Carol Elwood Graphic Design
Typographers: Total Graphics, Inc.
Photographer: Patricia L. Hirschy

Published by

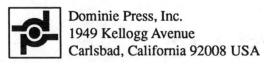

Dominie Press, Inc.
1949 Kellogg Avenue
Carlsbad, California 92008 USA

ISBN 1-56270-972-0
Printed in U.S.A.

Contents

National Holidays and Symbols

U.S. and State Capital

State and Local Government

Immigration and Naturalization

Appendices

Introduction

*T*he *Way to U.S. Citizenship* is a basic United States history and government workbook designed specifically for teaching ESL learners. It integrates two areas: **language** and **content**. Content and language are made more comprehensible to beginning and intermediate ESL learners by using proven pedagogical and linguistic devices to shelter the English language. The unique learning needs of the permanent resident and citizenship candidates have been recognized.

The Way to U.S. Citizenship acknowledges that permanent resident and citizenship candidates first need to be able to use language to pass required tests, as indicated by the INS. Later, they will need English to survive in an English-language setting. This text addresses fundamentally the primary need, without neglecting the other.

The Way to U.S. Citizenship provides learners with the knowledge and understanding of history and government of the United States that they need initially. Often, knowledge and understanding occur first on the comprehension level before students are able to produce. The **Activity Section** of each lesson presents comprehension and production exercises. The skills that are necessary to cope with the learner's present needs are immediately focused in the appropriate contexts.

The Way to U.S. Citizenship also recognizes the need for practice and repetition and for communication by means of dialogue. Learners work individually, in pairs, and in groups, thus acquiring the exchange of meaningful content information as well as the structures needed to comprehend and give information.

Finally, *The Way to U.S. Citizenship* acknowledges that adult learners have acquired and use their native language for various purposes daily. It also recognizes that a lack of knowledge of English is *not* synonymous with ignorance and that what learners already know in their native language may be used as a device to help them learn/acquire a second language. This text incorporates many of these tools.

To the Teacher

The Way to U.S. Citizenship includes features that teachers have requested for many years.

- It integrates language and content. Learners are provided with practice exercises that encompass both aspects.
- It makes abundant use of **true cognates.** Learners can recognize words that in their native language are similar in form and meaning to words in English. This facilitates comprehension.
- It uses structures that are more parallel to those in the learners' native language. Content is easier to grasp.
- It makes abundant use of structures in the active voice. Content is easier to understand.
- It provides practice with communicative structures. Learners acquire pertinent language practice.

- It provides useful appendices, which include a glossary of English-Spanish terms. Learners can use their knowledge of the first language to help them learn/acquire the second language.

Structure of the Workbook

The Way to U.S. Citizenship contains 36 lessons. Each lesson lists the respective objectives. This list of objectives is followed by a narrative, an activity section with various exercises, and a quiz.

Terms or expressions perceived to be difficult for learners are italicized, and the equivalent term as used in that particular context is provided in Spanish in Appendix 11. The teacher's task has been made easier, yet at the same time the content has been sheltered as much as possible to minimize the learner's apprehension and to facilitate his or her comprehension of the content.

An answer key is provided, which allows learners to work at home or in a classroom setting.

Presentation of the Material

The reading passage in each lesson provides content in a sheltered manner; however, students need to be prepared for oral-aural interaction.

As the instructor, you must present the material. It is suggested that you provide some simple practice with listening exercises before reading. Ask questions to which students may respond with one-word answers—true, false, give a number, give a date, give a name—or by raising one or several fingers. Once the reading passage has been introduced, give practice with the material. Practice different ways questions are asked:

Q: What is the highest law of the land?
A: The Constitution.
Q: What is the Constitution?
A: The highest law of the land.
Q: Who was the first president?
A: George Washington.
Q: Who was George Washington?
A: The first president.
Q: How long is a senator's term?
A: Six years.
Q: How long does a senator serve?
A: Six years.

Say true or false.
A: George Pataki is the governor of California.
B: False.
A: George Pataki is the governor of New York.
B: True.

Read a sentence and have students give the respective Wh-word for the question.
A: Bill Clinton is the president.
B: Who?
A: The president was reelected in 1996.
B: When?
Give group practice and assignments. Have one group obtain from another the information each does not have. Provide for individual, pair, and group work.

The Way to U.S. Citizenship provides a variety of exercises that will facilitate your already difficult task. It will help learners learn/acquire the language and content they need to become U.S. citizens.

Lesson 1
Maps and the World

Objectives

On completion of Lesson 1, students will be able to (**1**) identify common features of maps and (**2**) locate the United States on a map.

There are many kinds of maps. They show the *surface* of the earth. Some maps show countries. Some maps show states. Other maps show cities, mountains, and large areas of water.

A globe is one kind of map. It is a round map that shows the *whole* surface of the earth. The North Pole is at the top of the globe. The South Pole is at the bottom of the globe.

A surface map is another kind of map. A surface map is a flat map that shows the whole world or just one part of it. Surface maps are usually on paper. The maps in this book are surface maps. The top of the surface map is north, and the bottom is south. The right side of the surface map is east, and the left side is west.

The equator is *halfway* between the North Pole and the South Pole. The equator runs through South America, Africa, and parts of Southeast Asia. The equator cuts the world into two hemispheres: the *Northern Hemisphere* and the *Southern Hemisphere*. The world is also divided into two other hemispheres: the *Eastern Hemisphere* and the *Western Hemisphere*. The United States is in the Northern and Western Hemispheres.

Maps of the world show the seven continents on the surface of the earth. A continent is a very large area of land. The United States is on the continent of North America. The continent of North America also *includes* Canada and Mexico.

Maps of the world also show the four oceans. An ocean is a very large body of salt water. The United States is next to two oceans: the Atlantic Ocean and the Pacific Ocean.

Look at the map of the world in Appendix 1 and locate the United States on the map.

Activity Section

Activity 1

Match the two columns to complete each sentence.

1. A globe

2. Most surface maps

3. At the top of a globe

4. At the bottom of a globe

5. The right side of a surface map

6. The left side of a surface map

_6_ is west.

_3_ is the North Pole.

_1_ is a round map of the earth.

_5_ is east.

_2_ are on paper.

_4_ is the South Pole.

Activity 2

**Look at the map of the world in Appendix 1. Find the United States.
Then answer these questions.**

1. Which ocean is west of the United States?

PACIFIC

2. Which country is north of the United States?

CANADA

3. Which country is south of the United States?

MEXICO

4. Which ocean is east of the United States?

ATLANTIC

5. On which continent do you live?

NORTH AMERICAN

Activity 3 (pair or group work)

Ask a classmate the following questions. Then write the answers.

1. Which kinds of maps show the world?

   PAPER of SURFACE , GLOBE

2. Where is the equator?

   ½ bt ocean North & South Pole

3. Is a surface map round?

   No FLAT

4. How many hemispheres are there? _4_

5. How are surface maps and globes different?

   flat / round

6. Are there six oceans in the world? _4_

7. Which hemisphere is the United States in?

   NORTH / WEST

8. Which continent is the United States on?

   NORTH AMERICA

Quiz

Choose words from the box. Fill in the blanks to complete each sentence.

continents	globe	equator
oceans	Atlantic Ocean	pole
continent	south	

1. There are seven _continents_ in the world.

2. A _globe_ shows the whole surface of the earth.

3. The _Atlantic Ocean_ is a large body of water next to the U.S.

4. The bottom of a surface map is _south_ .

5. The _Equator_ is halfway between the North Pole and the South Pole.

6. There are four _oceans_ in the world.

7. The United States is on the _continent_ of North America.

Lesson 2
Columbus and the Native Americans

Objectives

On completion of Lesson 2, students will be able to (1) identify Columbus as the person who discovered America, (2) state the date Columbus discovered America, (3) identify the original inhabitants of the U.S., and (4) describe how the inhabitants lived.

Christopher Columbus was born in Genoa, Italy. He was a navigator. He sailed far north to England and far south to the Azores. He thought there was a shorter way to India if he crossed the Atlantic. Columbus studied the winds and currents of the ocean. He went to the king and queen of Spain with his ideas. They helped him.

In 1492, Christopher Columbus found the land we call America. Columbus wanted to find a shorter way to the Indies. The *king* and queen of Spain gave Columbus three ships for the trip. Columbus sailed west across the ocean until he came to land. Because he *thought* the land was the Indies, he called the people living there "Indians." Columbus was not in the Indies. He had found a land new to Europeans.

There were different groups of Indians. Each had different customs and languages. Some were *hunters*. Some were *fishermen* or *farmers*. The groups, or nations, had different kinds of houses and leaders. All of the nations took care of the land. They took from the land only what they needed.

Today we call the Indians "native Americans" because they were the first people to live on the North American continent.

Activity Section

Activity 1

Match the two columns to complete each sentence.

1. Before 1492, Europeans _____5_____ native Americans.

2. Christopher Columbus sailed _____4_____ Indians.

3. The king and queen of Spain _____6_____ different customs.

4. Columbus called the people living in America _____1_____ did not know about America.

5. Another name for Indians is _____2_____ west until he saw land.

6. The different nations had _____7_____ a shorter way to the Indies.

7. Columbus wanted to find _____3_____ gave Columbus three ships.

Activity 2

Complete these sentences.

The name of the man who found America is ___COLUMBUS___ .

The king and queen of ___SPAIN___ gave him ships to go to

the Indies. In the year ___1492___ , he sailed ___west___ and

found a new land. The people in the new land lived in groups called

___nation___ . We now call those people ___Native Americans___

because they were the first people to live on the continent of

___NORTH AMERICA___

Activity 3

Practice these sentences.

1. Who was **Columbus?**   **A navigator.**
            a navigator?   Columbus
            born in Genoa?   Columbus

2. Columbus sailed **far north to England.**
            far south to the Azores
            across the Atlantic

Quiz

Write <u>true</u> or <u>false</u> after each sentence.

1. Columbus called the people in North America "Indians." __T__

2. Columbus found the Indies before he went to North America. __F__

3. Columbus went east to find America. __F__

4. The Indians lived in one big group. __F__

5. Some of the Indians were hunters. __T__

6. The Indians took care of the land. __T__

7. We call Europeans "native Americans." __F__

8. Columbus sailed on ships to find America. __T__

NINA
PINTA
SANTA MARIA

Lesson 3
Explorers and Missionaries

Objectives

On completion of Lesson 3, students will be able to name two reasons why Europeans came to live in the New World.

After Columbus found America, many other Europeans came to the *New World.* Many people were *explorers.* They wanted to find gold and to *claim* land for their countries.

In the 1500s, the explorers from Spain claimed more land than the explorers from France or England. The Spanish explorers took the land from the Indians. The Spanish claimed the land in North America that is now Mexico and the southern part of the United States. The English and French explorers claimed smaller pieces of land that are now in Canada.

Amerigo Vespucci was an explorer for Spain and Portugal. He made a map of the New World and named the land "America."

The Spanish explorers claimed large portions of land in America. *Later,* they *sent* missionaries to the New World. The missionaries *built* missions and *taught* the Christian religion to the Indians. The missionaries *brought* horses, cows, and other animals with them. They were the first Europeans to live in North America.

People from other countries in Europe heard about America. These countries sent explorers to learn about the new land. These European countries also sent colonists to the New World. The English sent explorers. The Dutch sent explorers. The French sent explorers. John Cabot explored North America for England. Henry Hudson explored North America for the Netherlands and England. Jacques Cartier and Samuel Champlain explored North America for France.

Activity Section

Activity 1 (pair or group work)

Ask a classmate the following questions. Then write the answers.

1. Who gave the name "America" to the New World?

_____

2. Which European countries sent explorers to North America?

_____

3. Which explorers claimed more land in the 1500s?

_____

4. What did the missionaries teach the Indians?

_____

5. Who claimed land that is now part of Canada?

_____

Activity 2

Complete these sentences.

In the 1500s, many _____ came to the New World to find

gold. They took _____ from the Indians. The explorers

from _____ claimed more land than the explorers from

other countries. The first Europeans to live in North America were the

_____ . They wanted to teach _____ to

the Indians.

Activity 3

Practice these sentences.

1. The **Spaniards** sent **missionaries** and soldiers.

     French   explorers
     English   *preachers*

2. Who **taught religion?** The Europeans did.

     sent soldiers
     built missions
     claimed land
     brought animals

3. They wanted to **teach religion.**

     claim land
     find gold

4. What did Columbus find? He found **the New World.**

     land
     North America
     Indians

Quiz

Write the letter of the correct answer in the blank.

1. _____ claimed land for their country.
    a. Indians   b. Explorers   c. Missionaries

2. The explorers wanted to find _____ .
    a. gold   b. horses   c. Indians

3. Spain took land from the _____ .
    a. English   b. Indians   c. Europeans

4. People from _____ brought horses and cows to North America.
    a. Italy   b. India   c. Spain

5. Spain sent people to build _____ .
    a. missions   b. houses   c. ships

Lesson 4
English Colonies in the New World

Objectives
On completion of Lesson 4, students will be able to (1) give reasons why Europeans came to live in the New World and (2) identify the number of original colonies.

In the 1600s, many people came to America from England, France, and Spain. They came to America for different *reasons*. Some people came to America because they wanted *political freedom*. Some wanted *religious freedom*. Others wanted to *own* land or to find gold.

Some of the first people to arrive in the northeastern part of the colonies were from England. The English people *founded* the first two permanent colonies on the Atlantic coast: Jamestown and Plymouth.

The colony at Jamestown, Virginia, began in 1607. The London Company in England founded the colony to make money in the New World. Soon the *colonists* learned how to grow *tobacco*. They *grew* tobacco, *sold* the tobacco to people in Europe, and made a lot of money.

A group of people called the Pilgrims began the Plymouth colony. The Pilgrims did not have religious freedom in England, so they left England. They sailed to America on a ship called the Mayflower and arrived at Cape Cod in November 1620.

Life was not *easy* for the Pilgrims the first year in the new country, but the Indians helped them. The Indians taught the Pilgrims how to farm and how to grow corn and other *crops*. The Pilgrims had a celebration of *thanksgiving* with the Indians at the *end* of the first year. This celebration is now called Thanksgiving Day.

Soon the Indians and the Pilgrims *helped* each other, and they traded things they had or made.

Other people from Europe came to the New World. Some of them founded colonies on the eastern shore of America. Each colony made its own laws, and the people in the colony obeyed them. But the government of England *still controlled* most of the colonies. By 1750, there were 13 English colonies in North America: Connecticut, Delaware, Georgia, Maryland, Massachusetts, New Hampshire, New Jersey, New York, North Carolina, Pennsylvania, Rhode Island, South Carolina, and Virginia.

Activity Section

Activity 1

Practice these sentences.

1. **The Jamestown colonists** came to America in **1607.**
   The Pilgrims   1620
   My friends

2. Some colonists wanted to have **political freedom.**
                          religious freedom
                          land
                          a business

3. People came from **England.**
                     France
                     Spain
                     Mexico

4. **First,** there were **2** colonies.
   Later   more
   Then   13

5. The Indians taught the Pilgrims how to grow **corn.**
                                       crops
                                       tobacco
                                       other things

6. Did people come from **France?** Yes, they did.
                        Spain
                        England
                        Mexico

Activity 2

Match the two columns to complete each sentence.

1. Many people came to America from _3_ 13 English colonies.

2. Some people came to America for _6_ organized the Plymouth colony.

3. By 1750, there were _1_ England, France, and Spain.

4. Jamestown and Plymouth _2_ religious freedom.

5. The Pilgrims came to America _5_ on the Mayflower.

6. The Pilgrims _7_ in England.

7. There was no religious freedom _8_ its own laws.

8. Each colony had _9_ helped each other.

9. The Pilgrims and the Indians _4_ were the first permanent English colonies.

Quiz

Write _true_ or _false_ after each sentence.

1. All Europeans came to America to own a business. _F_

2. The Pilgrims came from England. _T_

3. Spanish people founded the first two permanent colonies in 1607. _F_

4. There were 13 colonies by 1750. _T_

5. The Pilgrims taught the Indians to grow crops. _F_

Lesson 5
The Colonists Were Unhappy

Objectives

On completion of Lesson 5, students will be able to (1) identify a reason for the colonists' rebellion and (2) name a given incident that caused the colonists to rebel.

The colonists were unhappy with English rule for many reasons. The most important reason was high taxes. England and France fought over the land in the New World. England *obtained most* of the land we know as the United States. But the war cost England a lot of money. The king of England *demanded* that the colonists pay high taxes to pay for the war *debt*.

The colonists enjoyed freedom when they helped the English against the French. But they were not happy with the high taxes, so they sent representatives of the 13 colonies to England. They wanted the representatives to defend their interests. The colonists *believed* that with their representatives present, they would get fair tax laws. The king of England did not accept the representatives from the colonies. When the colonists insisted on representation, the king made them pay higher taxes.

One of the colonists' famous protests against the English high taxes *was called* the Boston Tea Party. People in the colonies drank a lot of tea imported from England. The king placed a high tax on tea. This made the colonists very *angry*.

The colonists decided to take action. They wanted to protest *against* the *unjust* English tax on tea. One night a group of colonists *dressed* as native Americans and *quietly climbed* onto an English ship that was *loaded* with tea. They *threw* the tea over the *side* of the ship. This incident was called the Boston Tea Party. The colonists were *on their way* to rebellion. They wanted to be free from the unjust government of England.

Activity Section

Activity 1

Match the two columns to complete each sentence.

1. England and France ___3___ representatives to England.

2. The colonies were on their way ___6___ a lot of tea.

3. People in the colonies wanted to send ___2___ to rebellion.

4. The king did not accept ___9___ native Americans.

5. When the colonists insisted, the king ___4___ the colonists' representatives.

6. People in the colonies drank ___8___ very angry.

7. The king placed a ___7___ high tax on tea.

8. The colonists became ___5___ made them pay more taxes.

9. A group of men dressed up as ___10___ the Boston Tea Party.

10. This incident was called ___1___ fought a war.

Activity 2

Circle the correct response.

1. The king of England was _____B_____ .
   a. just   b. unjust

2. People in the colonies _____A_____ to pay taxes.
   a. did not like   b. liked

3. The king _____B_____ change the laws.
   a. did   b. did not

4. Colonists drank _____A_____ tea.
   a. a lot of   b. very little

5. The king placed _____A_____ on tea.
   a. a high tax   b. a low tax

Quiz

Answer the following questions. You can use short or complete answers.

1. Who paid a lot of taxes?

   COLONISTS

2. Who made them pay taxes?

   KING OF ENGLAND

3. The people wanted representation. Did the king accept?

   _NO_

4. Did the people insist?

   YES

5. Were the colonists happy?

   _NO_

6. Who dressed up as native Americans?

   COLONISTS

7. What did they do?

   CLIMBED ONTO AN ENGLISH SHIP & THREW TEA OVER THE SIDE

8. What do we call this incident?

   BOSTON TEA PARTY

Lesson 6
The Colonists and Freedom

Objectives

On completion of Lesson 6, students will be able to (1) identify July 4 as the birthday of the United States, (2) identify the name of the new country, and (3) identify who wrote most of the Declaration of Independence.

The colonists *suffered* under English law. They were angry because they *had to pay* high taxes and because the English *punished* them unjustly. Finally, the colonists wrote a Declaration of Rights. This document asked the king to *correct* the problems they complained about. The king did not listen.

The colonists called a meeting in Philadelphia to form a new government. They wanted to write their own laws and to declare their independence from England. They asked Thomas Jefferson to write the Declaration of Independence. On July 4, 1776, the members of the Convention signed the Declaration of Independence, which is based on the belief that all people are created equal. Americans celebrate July 4 as the birthday of the United States.

Since they declared their independence, the colonists prepared for war with the English army. They formed an army to fight for freedom. The colonists asked George Washington to lead the new American army.

Many men and boys from the 13 colonies joined George Washington and became part of Washington's army.

The War of Independence against England is also called the Revolutionary War. The colonists believed in freedom, and they fought *bravely* for it. Many *brave* men and women *died* during this war. They died for the freedom of all Americans. Their battle cry, which was first raised by a war hero named Patrick Henry, was, "Give me liberty or give me death."

After seven difficult years of *fighting,* Washington's army *won* the war. The free people called themselves Americans. The new country they called the United States of America.

Activity Section

Activity 1

Number the events in correct order.

1. _2_   The colonists wanted their own laws.

2. _1_   The colonists wanted freedom.

3. _3_   Thomas Jefferson wrote the Declaration of Independence.

4. _4_   The colonists signed the Declaration of Independence on July 4, 1776.

5. _6_   The colonists fought for at least seven years.

6. _7_   They called the new country the United States of America.

7. _5_   Many people died during the war.

Activity 2

Choose words from the box. Fill in the blanks to complete each sentence.

Jefferson	birthday
freedom	Washington
Revolutionary War	Declaration

1. The colonists wanted _Freedom_ .

2. _Jeff_ wrote an important document.

3. July 4 is America's _BIRTHDAY_ .

4. _WASH_ led the American army.

5. Colonists fought the _REVODGU_ .

6. The important document was the _DECLARE_ of Independence.

Quiz

Circle the correct response.

1. America's birthday is _____ .
   a. July 6, 1774   (b.) July 4, 1776

2. _____ wrote the Declaration of Independence.
   a. George Washington   (b.) Thomas Jefferson

3. The War of Independence is _____ .
   (a.) the Revolutionary War   b. the Indian War

4. The colonists _____ .
   (a.) fought bravely   b. did not fight bravely

5. The colonists fought for _____ .
   a. 17 years   (b.) 7 years

Lesson 7
The First Government

Objectives

On completion of Lesson 7, students will be able to **(1)** identify the Articles of Confederation as a plan of government and **(2)** state the purpose of the Constitutional Convention.

When the colonies were *no longer* governed by the king of England, they formed a new government. The new government faced many problems. One of these problems was the different interests of the states. Another problem was that most people did not want *centralized government.* They wanted the states and the people to control government directly. Delegates met in Philadelphia for the Continental Congress and wrote the Articles of Confederation. This document was the basis of a plan of government.

In 1787, the 13 states sent representatives to Philadelphia to a new convention to revise the Articles of Confederation. To make their jobs *easier,* the representatives wrote the Preamble. It begins with the words "We the People of the United States . . . " It *promised* to *protect* the liberty and rights of the people and to establish a Constitution. It was a difficult job. The representatives *disagreed* over equal representation and the balance of *power*

among the states. They especially disagreed over the power of the federal government. The representatives worked hard at the convention. When they completed their work and agreed on the new form of government, they wrote the new Constitution.

It was not easy to convince the states to *approve* the new Constitution. At first, the states did not want to give up their power to a central government, but they wanted a unified country; finally they agreed. The people in each state voted in favor of the new Constitution. With the approval of the Constitution by all 13 states, the people of America had a new Constitution and a new republic. Under a republican form of government, the power is held by citizens who vote for people to represent them. These representatives exercise the power, but they must answer to the people.

Activity Section

Activity 1

Circle the correct response.

1. There were representatives of _____ at the new convention.
   a. 12 states   (b.) 13 states

2. The states _____ over the power of the central government.
   a. agreed   (b.) disagreed

3. The new convention wrote _____ .
   (a.) the Articles of Confederation   b. the new Constitution

4. The new government _____ .
   (a.) faced many problems   b. had no problems

5. All the states _____ the Constitution immediately.
   a. approved   (b.) did not approve

6. All _____ states approved the Constitution.
   a. 12   (b.) 13

Activity 2

Write <u>true</u> or <u>false</u> after each sentence.

1. It was easy to approve the new Constitution.   _F_

2. Colonists wrote the Preamble after they wrote the Constitution.   _F_

3. The Preamble protected the liberty and rights of the people.   _T_

4. All 13 states approved the Constitution.   _T_

5. The states disagreed over equal representation.   _T_

Activity 3

Practice these sentences.

1. The **convention** approved the **Preamble.**

    delegates   Preamble

    delegates   Constitution

    people   Constitution

2. The **representatives** worked hard.

    convention

    people

3. Some states wanted **equal representation.**

        federal government

        total independence

        a new form of government

Quiz

Answer the following questions. Use short or complete answers.

1. What are the Articles of Confederation?

_____

2. In what year was the Constitutional Convention?

_____

3. What was the basis of a plan of government?

_____

4. What was the *purpose* of the Constitutional Convention?

_____

5. The new government faced many problems. Name two.

_____

Lesson 8
The Constitution

Objectives

On completion of Lesson 8, students will be able to **(1)** state the year the Constitution was written, **(2)** identify the Constitution as a plan of government, and **(3)** identify the Constitution as the highest law of the land.

The leaders of the 13 states met in Philadelphia, Pennsylvania, in 1787 to write the United States Constitution. Famous men *attended* the Constitutional Convention, among them John Adams, Benjamin Franklin, Thomas Jefferson, and James Madison. James Madison is called the Father of the Constitution, because as the secretary of the Convention, he wrote most of it.

A constitution is a plan of government. The colonists wanted to *ensure* that the government would be by the people, of the people, and for the people. The Constitution was so important that it became the supreme law of the land. The Constitution is above all state constitutions.

The writers of the Constitution divided the document into three parts: the Preamble, the Articles, and the Amendments.

The Preamble begins with the words "We the People of the United States . . . " The Preamble is the introduction to the Constitution. It states that the Constitution is necessary to (a) form a united country, (b) *establish* justice, (c) *insure* peace and order,

(d) promote general *welfare,* and (e) secure liberty for ourselves and for others.

The second section of the Constitution is the Articles. These articles indicate the structure of government. It separates the structure of the government into three branches: the executive branch, the legislative branch, and the judicial branch. Each branch has special powers and responsibilities. The executive branch *enforces* the laws. The legislative branch makes the laws. The judicial branch explains the laws. Each branch watches over the power and the responsibilities of the other two branches. These checks and balances protect the rights of citizens and noncitizens living in the United States.

The third section of the Constitution is the Amendments. There are two parts to the Amendments. The first ten amendments are called the Bill of Rights. The rest, numbers 11 to 27, are called amendments. The Bill of Rights guarantees our basic rights. The last amendments were added to protect those rights not covered by the Bill of Rights.

Activity Section

Activity 1 (pair work)

Practice the dialogue with another student.

S-1: What is a constitution?

S-2: It is a plan of government.

S-1: *Tell* me about the United States Constitution.

S-2: It is the highest law of the country.

S-1: Is "the highest law" the same as "the supreme law"?

S-2: Yes, highest and supreme mean the *same* thing.

S-1: That was very interesting. Thanks.

S-2: You're welcome.

Activity 2

Match the two columns to complete each sentence.

1. The United States Constitution is the   6   is a plan of government.

2. Every state has a   4   the government must have three branches.

3. The United States Constitution is above   2   state constitution.

4. The United States Constitution says that   5   control the whole government.

5. One branch of government cannot   1   supreme law of the land.

6. A constitution   3   all state constitutions.

Activity 3

Fill in the blanks.

1. The legislative branch _____*makes*_____ the laws.

2. The executive branch _____*enforces*_____ the laws.

3. The judicial branch _____*explains*_____ the laws.

Quiz

Circle the correct response.

1. The supreme law of the United States _____ .
   a. is the Constitution   b. are state constitutions

2. The United States Constitution is _____ all state constitutions.
   a. below   b. above

3. The Constitution divided the government into _____ branches.
   a. two   b. three

4. One branch cannot _____ the whole government.
   a. control   b. divide

5. A constitution is a _____ of government.
   a. place   b. plan

6. The three branches of government are _____ .
   a. the police, the army, and   b. the legislative, the judicial, and
      the navy   the executive

Lesson 9
The Three Branches of Government

Objectives

On completion of Lesson 9, students will be able to (1) name the three branches of government and (2) identify what each branch of government does.

The government consists of three main branches: the executive branch, the legislative branch, and the judicial branch. Each branch is *separate* and has special powers. Each watches over the other.

The legislative branch, or Congress, has two parts: the Senate and the House of Representatives. Each state elects members to the House of Representatives in proportion to the number of people living in the state. States with more people have a greater voice in the House of Representatives. The principal function of the legislators is to make laws.

The executive branch consists of the following members: the president, the vice president, the secretaries of the cabinet, and the heads of federal agencies. The main function of the executive branch is to *enforce* the laws that the legislature makes.

The judicial branch consists of the Supreme Court and various federal courts, such as district courts and circuit courts of appeal. The Supreme Court is the highest court in the country.

The persons who decide cases in the judicial branch are judges. The principal *responsibility* of the judicial branch is to explain the law.

In 1787, the writers of the Constitution wanted all 13 states and all future states to have the same form of government. All states in the Union have the same structure of government: an executive branch, a legislative branch, and a judicial branch.

The separation of powers creates a balance of power. Each branch has its own function and its own responsibility. Each checks and balances the power of the other two branches to protect the rights of the people.

Activity Section

Activity 1

Circle the correct response.

1. The government has _____ parts, or branches.
   a. four   b. three

2. The legislative branch _____ laws.
   a. makes   b. enforces

3. The executive branch _____ laws.
   a. makes   b. enforces

4. The judicial branch _____ laws.
   a. makes   b. explains

5. The Senate is in the _____ branch.
   a. executive   b. legislative

6. The House of Representatives is in the _____ branch.
   a. executive   b. legislative

7. The president works in the _____ branch.
   a. executive   b. judicial

8. The Supreme Court works in the _____ branch.
   a. executive   b. judicial

9. The vice president works in the _____ branch.
   a. executive   b. judicial

10. The separation of power creates _____ .
    a. checks and balances   b. laws

Activity 2 (pair work)

Practice this interview with another student.

INS Agent: Good afternoon, Mrs. Torres.

Applicant: Good afternoon, Officer Peters.

INS Agent: Are you ready for some questions on government?

Applicant: Yes, I think so.

INS Agent: Okay. Let's see. How many branches are in the government?

Applicant: Three.

INS Agent: Can you name them?

Applicant: Yes. The legislative, the executive, and the judicial.

INS Agent: Where does the president work?

Applicant: He works in the executive branch.

INS Agent: What does the judicial branch do?

Applicant: It explains the laws.

INS Agent: How is the legislative branch divided?

Applicant: The legislative branch has two parts: the House of Representatives and the Senate.

INS Agent: Who is the president of the United States of America?

Applicant: He is William Jefferson Clinton.

INS Agent: Very good, Mrs. Torres. Those are all the questions. You knew the answers very well. Congratulations. I will recommend you for permanent residency.

Applicant: Thank you, Officer Peters. The questions were very easy. I was very nervous. I was afraid I would *fail*.

Quiz

Write <u>true</u> or <u>false</u> after each sentence.

1. The executive branch controls the legislative branch and the judicial branch.   _f_

2. Judges are members of the legislative branch.   _f_

3. Every state has equal numbers of representatives.   _f_

4. The Supreme Court is the highest court in the country.   _T_

5. The president and vice president elect the legislative branch.   _f_

Lesson 10
The Executive Branch

Objectives

On completion of Lesson 10, students will be able to (**1**) identify qualifications to become president and vice president, (**2**) state the duration of the terms for president and vice president, and (**3**) name the branch in which the president and vice president work.

The executive branch consists of the president, the vice president, the secretaries of the cabinet, and the heads of independent agencies. The main responsibility of the executive branch is to enforce the laws that Congress writes. It is also the duty of the president to watch over the judicial and legislative branches.

The president is the leader of the nation and the commander in chief of the *armed forces*. The president *runs* the country with the help of the vice president and the cabinet. They are the president's advisors.

To be president, a person must be a native-born citizen, at least 35 years old, and a resident of the United States for at least 14 years. The vice president can become president if the president dies or is ill. Therefore, the same set of qualifications applies to the vice president. If both the president and the vice president become ill or die, then the speaker of the House of Representatives becomes president.

The Constitution *allows* presidents to be reelected only once. The term of office is four years. At the end of the four years, the president can run for reelection. Amendment 22 of the Constitution says that a president cannot run for three terms in office. This protects the country from a possible *dictatorship*.

The vice president presides over the Senate. He votes only in case of a tie.

The cabinet members advise the president on certain policy matters. They help the president carry out policies.

The independent agencies provide special services. They also help the president carry out policies.

Activity Section

Activity 1

Choose words from the box. Fill in the blanks to complete each sentence.

```
       native American          four years
       executive branch         enforces
       native-born              writes
       reelected
```

1. Independent agencies are part of the _____ .

2. The president is a _____ citizen.

3. The president's term is for _____ .

4. The Constitution allows presidents to be _____ .

5. Congress _____ the laws.

6. The president _____ the laws.

Activity 2

Practice these sentences.

1. Who **makes** the laws? **The legislative branch.**

    enforces   The executive branch.
    explains   The judicial branch.

2. Who is the **head of the executive branch?** The president.

            leader of the nation
            chief of the armed forces
            chief executive

3. The president must be a **native citizen.**

                at least 35 years old
                of good moral character
                a leader

Quiz

Circle the correct response.

1. The vice president of the United States is _____ years old.
   a. at least 21   (b.) at least 35

2. The president is the _____ .
   a. leader of Congress   (b.) leader of the nation

3. The president's term of office is _____ .
   (a.) four years   b. eight years

4. The president _____ be reelected once.
   (a.) can   b. cannot

5. The _____ is the commander of the armed forces.
   a. vice president   (b.) president

6. The president and vice president work in the _____ .
   a. legislative branch   (b.) executive branch

Lesson 11
The President

Objectives

On completion of Lesson 11, students will be able to **(1)** identify two of the president's responsibilities and **(2)** identify how a president is elected by the electoral vote.

The president of the United States is the chief executive of the government. It is the president's duty to enforce the laws of the country with help from the cabinet and the independent federal agencies. The president has a variety of duties to keep the government functioning. It is the president's responsibility to work with the legislative and judicial branches. The president also conducts foreign policy. The president is the head, or the commander in chief, of the armed forces. One of the special duties of the president is to nominate judges to the Supreme Court. The president also nominates officials to the cabinet or federal agencies, but these officials must receive approval by the Senate.

As part of the check over Congress, the president can refuse to sign, or veto, a bill passed by Congress. The president can also pardon a person found guilty of a federal crime. The president can change the course of history while in office.

Every four years there is a presidential election. Political parties choose presidential candidates for the election. There have been many political parties in the United States. The two major political parties today are the Democratic Party and the Republican Party. To choose their candidates, political parties have conventions in every state. Members of each party vote for the candidate they prefer. Each party has a national convention to select candidates for president and vice president. Independent candidates may also run for office.

General elections are in November. There is a "popular" vote and an "electoral" vote. The popular vote is the actual number of people voting for a candidate. The electoral vote is decided by the number of representatives and senators each state has in the federal government. The District of Columbia also has three electoral votes. There is a total of 538 electoral votes. The candidate with the majority of the popular votes in a state usually wins all of the electoral votes for that state. These votes are cast in the state capitals in December. The results are sent to Washington, D.C. and are counted in Congress in January. A candidate needs a majority, or 270 electoral votes, to win an election. Because of electronic counting, the results of the general election are often known in November. But the new president's inauguration, or swearing-in ceremony, does not take place until January.

Activity Section

Activity 1

Match the two columns to complete each sentence.

1. The cabinet and independent agencies __2__ the president.

2. It takes 270 or more electoral votes to elect __6__ the popular vote.

3. The president's duty is to __4__ approves or rejects judges.

4. The Senate __3__ enforces laws.

5. The president can __1__ help the president.

6. The actual number of people voting is __5__ veto a bill passed by the Congress.

Activity 2

Circle the correct response.

1. The president of the United States is the ____b____ of the government.
   a. judge   b. chief executive

2. Every ____a____ years there is a presidential election.
   a. four   b. six

3. The popular vote is the actual number of ____a____ voting for a candidate.
   a. people   b. senators

4. A candidate needs a majority, or ____b____ electoral votes, to win an election.
   a. 4   b. 270

5. The District of Columbia has ____b____ electoral votes.
   a. six   b. three

6. The president has ____a____ .
   a. a variety of duties   b. one duty

Quiz

Answer the following questions.

1. Who is the chief executive of the United States?

    _____PRES_____

2. In what month is the general election held?

    _____NOVEMBER_____

3. Can the president conduct foreign policy?

    _____YES_____

4. Name the two major political parties.

    _____DEMOC____REP._____

5. The president is the commander in chief of what?

    _____ARMED FORCES_____

Lesson 12
The Cabinet and Federal Agencies

Objectives

On completion of Lesson 12, students will be able to (**1**) identify the role of the cabinet and independent agencies, (**2**) name two cabinet departments, and (**3**) name at least two independent federal agencies.

The president has many responsibilities To *carry out* these responsibilities, the president appoints many heads of executive departments. There are two main departments that help the president: the cabinet and the independent federal agencies.

Today, there are 14 federal departments in the president's cabinet. Each department has a head. The heads of these departments are called secretaries. The only exception is the head of the Department of Justice, who is called the attorney general. The Constitution does not call for a cabinet. However, beginning with George Washington, all the presidents have appointed people to these positions.

The 14 departments are (1) State, (2) *Treasury,* (3) Defense, (4) Justice, (5) Interior, (6) Agriculture, (7) Commerce, (8) Labor, (9) *Health and Human Services,* (10) Housing and Urban Development, (11) Transportation, (12) Education,

(13) Energy, and (14) Veterans Affairs. Each department has its responsibilities. Some departments are better known than others. For example, the Treasury Department collects taxes; the Justice Department enforces immigration; Health and Human Services administers Social Security and Welfare; Agriculture *gives out* food stamps and food.

There are many different independent federal agencies. Only a few are mentioned here. The U.S. Postal Service *delivers* millions of letters every day. The *Small Business* Administration advises and gives loans to small businesses. The Commission on Civil Rights watches over the civil rights of all citizens.

Activity Section

Activity 1

Circle the correct response.

1. The Treasury Department _____ A _____ .
   a. collects taxes   b. collects immigrants

2. The Health and Human Services Department _____ A _____ .
   a. administers Social Security   b. gives out food

3. The Agriculture Department _____ A _____ .
   a. gives out food   b. enforces immigration

4. The Postal Service is _____ A _____ .
   a. an independent federal   b. a department
      agency

5. The Small Business Administration gives _____ b _____ .
   a. business to small people   b. loans to small businesses

6. The Commission on Civil Rights is _____ B _____ .
   a. part of the Justice   b. an independent federal
      Department   agency

Activity 2

Practice these sentences.

What does the **Small Business Administration** do? **Advises small businesses.**

Postal Service	Delivers mail.
Federal Trade Commission	Promotes fair competition.
Civil Rights Commission	Watches over civil rights.

Activity 3 (pair work)

Ask a classmate the following questions. Then write the answers.

1. How many cabinet departments are there today?

   _____14_____

2. What is the head of each department called?

   _____Sec_____

3. Name two departments.

   _____

4. The attorney general is the head of a department. What is the department?

   _____

5. Name two independent federal agencies.

   _____U.S. Postal_____S.B.A._____

Quiz

Write <u>true</u> or <u>false</u> after each sentence.

1. Cabinets are independent agencies.   f

2. There are 14 federal departments in the president's cabinet.   t

3. The heads of departments are called secretaries.   t

4. The attorney general is the head of a department.   t

5. The U.S. Postal Service is a federal department.   f

Lesson 13
The Legislative Branch

Objectives

On completion of Lesson 13, students will be able to (**1**) identify the two houses of Congress and name the branch in which they are located and (**2**) state the number of senators elected in each state.

The writers of the Constitution wanted a form of government that would give equal power to small and large states. They wanted to protect the people from dictators. The division of the legislature protects the rights of individual states. The division of power between the branches protects the people from dictators. To keep balance of power between states, the *framers* of the Constitution established two different houses in the legislature: the Senate and the House of Representatives.

Each state elects two persons to the Senate. These persons are called senators. In the Senate, small states have equal power with larger states. This gives the states an equal opportunity to pass laws that benefit them.

Today the House of Representatives has over 435 members. Each state elects representatives in proportion to the number of people in the state. States are divided into congressional districts. Each district elects a representative. There is a census every ten years to count the population.

The main function of the legislature, or Congress, is to pass laws and to ensure that both the executive branch and the judicial branch keep *within* their *authority*.

The people of the U.S. give their representatives the power to make laws. The Senate and the House of Representatives work together as the Congress of the United States. The writers of the Constitution wanted two separate groups to approve the laws. They did not want laws passed hurriedly or carelessly. One house checks on the other. The House and the Senate are part of the "System of checks and balances" of power.

In 1992, some states limited terms in office.

Activity Section

Activity 1

Refer to the *passage* to complete this exercise.

The writers of the Constitution ___*wanted*___ a government that

would give ___*equal power*___ to large and small ___*states*___ .

The division of the ___*legislature*___ protects the rights of individual

___*states*___ . The division of power between the branches

___*protects*___ the people from ___*dictator*___ .

    Each state elects ___2___ persons to the Senate. Each state

elects representatives ___*in proportion*___ to the number of people in the state.

Activity 2

Match the two columns to answer each question.

1. What keeps the balance of power between the states?   __4__ 435

2. How many senators does each state elect?   __3__ the Senate and the
                                              House of Representatives

3. What are the two houses of Congress called?   __1__ the division of the legislature

4. How many members are there in the House today?   __2__ two

5. What is the main function of Congress?   __6__ 100

6. How many senators are there?   __5__ pass laws

Quiz

Circle the correct response.

1. The Senate and the House are part of _____*b*_____ .
   a. the executive branch   (b.) the legislative branch

2. Each state has _____*b*_____ .
   a. two representatives   b. at least one representative

3. There is a census _____*b*_____ .
   a. every four years   (b.) every ten years

4. In the Senate, large states have _____*a*_____ small states.
   a. equal power to   b. more power than

5. The legislature _____*a*_____ the executive branch.
   a. watches   b. controls

Capitol Building, Washington, D.C.

Lesson 14
The Senate

Objectives

On completion of Lesson 14, students will be able to (1) identify qualifications to become a senator and (2) identify functions of a senator.

The Senate is the smaller of the two houses of Congress. It has 100 members. The House and the Senate *share* the responsibility of making laws. Each of these houses also has a separate responsibility. The House *introduces* bills about the budget or taxes. The House also *impeaches* officials. The Senate determines the innocence or guilt of the impeached officials. It also confirms or denies *appointments* the president makes. Another function of the Senate is to *ratify treaties* between the U.S. and other governments. Each state elects two senators. To be a senator, a person must be at least 30 years old and a native or naturalized citizen. A *candidate* for senator must also be a citizen for at least nine years. A senator must live in the state he or she wants to represent.

As a part of Congress, senators have the responsibility to check and balance the power of the executive and judicial branches. Senators can make laws to collect *taxes* or *print* money. They can make laws on naturalization. Only the Senate along with the House of Representatives can declare *war*.

People elect senators for longer terms than representatives. They are elected for six-year terms. Some states have limited a senator to two terms in office. Often, senators gain *seniority* and become heads of committees that distribute money to different programs. A state can benefit *greatly* if one of its senators is the head of an important committee.

Citizens choose senators at a national election This election is held in November of each even-numbered year. In this way the Senate never has only new senators. The Senate always has a 2/3 majority of experienced senators.

See Appendix 4 for the names of U.S. senators. Learn the names of the U.S. senators from your state.

Activity Section

Activity 1

Circle the best answer in each case based on the passage.

1. Each state elects _____ *c* _____ .
   a. one senator   b. many senators   c. two senators

2. Senators must _____ *b* _____ .
   a. have money   b. be a resident of that state   c. live anywhere in the U.S.

3. Senators may be _____ *b* _____ .
   a. permanent residents   (b.) naturalized citizens   c. 29 years old

4. Senators may _____ *a* _____ .
   a. confirm appointments   b. make appointments   c. run the government

5. The main function of the Senate is _____ *b* _____ .
   a. to make money   b. to make laws   c. to collect taxes

Activity 2

Practice these sentences.

1. Who **writes laws?** Senators do.
   confirms appointments
   ratifies treaties
   rejects appointments

2. A senator must be **at least 30 years old.**
   a citizen at least nine years
   a resident of that state

3. The Senate **makes laws.**
   ratifies treaties
   approves appointments
   rejects appointments

Activity 3 (pair work)

Practice the dialogue with another student.

S-1:   I want to be a senator one day.

S-2:   Are you a naturalized citizen?

S-1:   Not yet, but I'll be a resident.

S-2:   Senators must be citizens.

S-1:   Then I'll be a citizen.

S-2:   How old are you?

S-1:   I'm 25 years old

S-2:   You have to be at least 30 years old.

S-1:   Then I'll wait.

Quiz

Answer the following questions. Use short or complete answers.

1. Are you a permanent resident?

   _____ Yes _____

2. How old are you?

   _____ 45 _____

3. Where do you live? (state) .

   _____

4. How long is a senator's term?

   _____ 6 yr _____

5. What is a senator's main function?

   _____ Make Law _____

Lesson 15
The House of Representatives

Objectives

On completion of Lesson 15, students will be able to **(1)** identify the qualifications to become a representative and **(2)** identify functions of the House of Representatives.

The House of Representatives is the larger of the two houses of Congress. Every district in a state elects members to the House of Representatives. In this part of the legislature, states with large populations have more power than states with small populations. This provides some balance of power between the states.

Most states are divided into districts, and each district chooses a representative. Every ten years, the government has a census to count the number of people per district throughout the country. States can either lose or gain representatives every ten years.

As part of Congress, the House of Representatives *shares* legislative responsibilities with the Senate. Their main responsibility is to write laws. Another responsibility is to watch and check the power of the executive and judicial branches. Like the senators, representatives can regulate money and trade. This function includes authorization to print money, to borrow money, to place and collect taxes, and to regulate trade between the states. Representatives and senators also share other responsibilities. They provide money to maintain the army, navy, and air force. They also make laws about naturalization of *aliens;* they *regulate* the system of *weights* and *measures;* they pass laws to govern the District of Columbia. Senators and representatives may also declare war. To be a representative, a person must be a citizen for at least seven years, at least 25 years old, and a resident of the state he or she represents. Representatives serve for two years. This means they have to campaign every two years.

In 1992 many states began limiting the term of office for their representatives. Most have agreed to limit them to three terms of two years each for a total of six years. Senior representatives often become heads of committees. They may help their state to get more money. These representatives may also help to pass laws that benefit the people in their states.

Activity Section

Activity 1

Match the two columns to complete each sentence.

1. The House of Representatives   _7_ can declare war.

2. Each district of a state   _4_ divided into districts.

3. States with smaller populations   _5_ every ten years.

4. Most states are   _2_ elects representatives.

5. There is a census   _6_ every two years.

6. There is an election for representatives   _8_ of people in the country.

7. The Senate and the House of Representatives   _3_ have fewer representatives.

8. A census counts the number   _1_ is the larger of the two houses of Congress.

Activity 2

Write <u>true</u> or <u>false</u> after each sentence.

1. The people elect representatives every six years. _F_

2. Each district elects representatives. _T_

3. The House of Representatives has fewer members than the Senate. _F_

4. States with smaller populations have fewer representatives. _T_

5. The number of representatives is always the same. _F_

Activity 3

Practice these sentences.

1. Representatives and senators **share responsibilities.**

> regulate trade
> provide money
> make laws

2. Every **four** years we elect a **president.**

two	representative
six	senator
four	governor

Quiz

Circle the correct response.

1. A representative must be at least _____*b*_____ .
   a. 30 years old   (b.) 25 years old

2. A representative must be a citizen for at least _____*b*_____ .
   a. nine years   b. seven years

3. Representatives _____*a*_____ .
   a. introduce bills   b. command the armed forces

4. Most states are divided into _____*b*_____ .
   a. provinces   b. districts

5. The House shares legislative responsibilities with _____*b*_____ .
   a. the president   b. the Senate

Lesson 16
From Bills to Laws

Objectives

On completion of Lesson 16, students will be able to (1) explain how a bill becomes a law in simple terms and (2) give two examples of checks or balance of power.

Only Congress can make laws. A law can begin in either the Senate or the House of Representatives. However, only representatives can introduce tax or budget *bills*. A bill begins with the idea for a law. The *procedure* for a bill to become law is not only complicated, but also very political.

If a senator or a representative has an idea for a law, he or she presents the bill to a committee. The committee may do one of four things. It can *amend*, or change, the bill. If the committee does not like it, it can *rewrite* the bill. If it wants to *kill* the bill, the committee ignores it. But if the committee likes the bill, it sends it to its house of Congress for debate.

When one of the houses gets the bill, it can do a number of things with it. Many times, different representatives or senators amend the bill. Sometimes representatives have debates about the bill for long periods. Finally, they vote to pass or to defeat it. If the first house passes a bill, it goes to the other house.

The other house must go through the *same procedure* as the first house to try to pass a bill. It begins as a bill in a committee. Then, if amended and passed, it is sent to the full house. There, the other legislators debate over the bill. Sometimes legislators amend a bill. When they do, they may *add* their favorite *items* to it. Finally, the second house must vote on the bill. Both houses must approve bills.

Even if both houses approve a bill, it is not law. The president has to sign the bill before it becomes law. The president may do one of three things. If the president signs the bill, it becomes law. The president may ignore the bill. Then if Congress *stays* in session, this bill becomes law. If Congress does not stay in session, it does not become law. The president may also v*eto* the bill. Then it does not become law. This is the president's check of Congress's power. Congress can approve a bill over the veto of the president. To do this requires 2/3 votes of both houses. This is Congress's check of the president's power.

Activity Section

Activity 1

Write <u>true</u> or <u>false</u> after each sentence.

1. Only the Senate can make laws. _____

2. The procedure for a bill to become law is very political. _____

3. To amend a bill means to make changes. _____

4. The president must sign every bill. _____

5. A bill must pass both houses. _____

Activity 2 (pair or group work)

Ask a classmate the following questions. Then write the answers.

1. Who makes laws?

_____

2. Can a woman be a senator?

_____

3. A committee may do one of four things about a bill. Name all four.

_____

4. Who introduces tax or budget bills?

_____

5. The president can check Congress's power. How?

_____

Activity 3

Indicate the order in which bills are approved.

_____ The committee can change, rewrite, kill, or send the bill to its house.

_____ The bill goes to the other house.

_____ The second house sends the bill to the president.

_____ Representatives present bills to a committee.

_____ The president signs or vetoes the bill.

_____ The second house also approves the bill.

Quiz

Circle the correct response.

1. An idea for a law is _____ .
   a. a bill   b. an appeal

2. To change a bill is to _____ .
   a. amend it   b. ignore it

3. To pass a bill is to _____ .
   a. kill it   b. approve it

4. Congress can pass a law over the president's veto with _____ of the
   votes from both houses.
   a. 2/3   b. 100%

5. _____ checks and balances between the executive and legislative
   branches.
   a. There are not   b. There are

Lesson 17
The Judicial Branch

Objectives

On completion of Lesson 17, students will be able to **(1)** name the branch in which the Supreme Court works, **(2)** identify the Supreme Court as the highest court in the land, **(3)** identify the function of the judicial branch, and **(4)** identify the right to appeal.

The federal court system is the main part of the judicial branch. The responsibility of the judicial branch is to explain and interpret the laws. The federal courts not only interpret the laws, but also judge the most important cases.

The Supreme Court is a part of the judicial branch. Nine persons serve on this court. The nine persons who serve on the Supreme Court are called Supreme Court justices. The Chief Justice of the Supreme Court is William Rehnquist. The Supreme Court justices interpret and decide how the Constitution applies to cases. It is the highest court in the land, and its decisions are final.

The Supreme Court checks and balances the power of the legislative and executive branches. It *ensures* that they both keep within the Constitutional *requirements*. Although the president *nominates* Supreme Court justices, Congress must approve their *nominations*. If approved, the justices serve for life.

It would be impossible for the Supreme Court to hear all cases. *Therefore,* there are different levels of courts. There are local, state, and federal courts. These courts give all *accused* a just *hearing*. A case may be heard in one of the district courts, in a circuit court, or finally in the Supreme Court.

Every person has the *right* to a just and *speedy* trial. If a person is accused of a federal crime, he or she is judged in one of the 94 district courts in the country. If the *lawyer* and the accused do not agree with the *verdict,* or decision, they can *appeal* to a higher court called the circuit court. If they still believe that the verdict is unjust and *wrong,* they can appeal to the Supreme Court. When the Supreme Court makes a decision, that decision is final. The Supreme Court is the highest court in the land. No one may appeal its decision.

Activity Section

Activity 1

Choose words from the box. Fill in the blanks to complete each sentence.

local	judicial	justices
other	explains	final

1. There are federal, state, and _____ courts.

2. The federal court system is the main part of the _____ branch.

3. There are nine _____ on the Supreme Court.

4. The judicial branch _____ the laws.

5. The Supreme Court checks and balances the power of the _____

   branches.

6. Supreme Court decisions are _____ .

Activity 2 (pair work)

Practice the dialogue with another student.

S-1: Hi Susana, what's the matter?

S-2: They accused Marcos of a crime.

S-1: Is he guilty?

S-2: Of course he isn't!

S-1: What are you going to do?

S-2: I will fight it in court. This is the United States.

S-1: That's right. Here you are innocent until *proven* guilty.

S-2: I'll get a good lawyer.

S-1: Good idea.

Activity 3 (pair or group work)

Ask a classmate the following questions. Then write the answers.

1. Who nominates Supreme Court justices?

_____

2. Who approves the nomination of Supreme Court justices?

_____

3. How long do Supreme Court justices serve?

_____

4. How many Supreme Court justices are there?

_____

5. You do not agree with a court decision. What can you do?

_____

6. Which is the highest court in the land?

_____

Quiz

Write true or false after each sentence.

1. The Supreme Court is a part of the executive branch.   _____

2. The Supreme Court is the highest court of the land.   _____

3. The judicial branch explains and interprets the laws.   _____

4. Supreme Court verdicts are final.   _____

5. Congress nominates Supreme Court justices.   _____

6. Supreme Court justices serve for life.   _____

7. Judges cannot sentence a person without a trial.   _____

Lesson 18
The First Four Presidents

Objectives

On completion of Lesson 18, students will be able to (1) identify George Washington as the first president of the United States, (2) identify Thomas Jefferson as the third president of the United States, and (3) identify Thomas Jefferson as the person who wrote the Declaration of Independence.

The United States had some great leaders as first presidents. George Washington, Thomas Jefferson, and James Madison were presidents in the early years. They were great leaders. John Adams was also one of our early presidents. The founders of this nation admired George Washington for his leadership qualities. He led his men on many missions during the French and Indian War. Later, when the colonies *held* the first Continental Congress, he was sent as a delegate to represent Virginia. The delegates recognized Washington's military experience and named him Commander of the Revolutionary Army. He and his men fought hard against the experienced English army and won the war.

Washington's work for his country did not end with the war. He was sent as a delegate to the Constitutional Convention held in Pennsylvania. As a *respected* leader of the group, he helped the delegates reach agreement on the Constitution. He was so highly respected that the people of the nation elected him the first president of the United States. President Washington decided to retire from politics after his second term. Washington was a great leader because he led his nation not only in war, but also in peace.

John Adams was the second president of the United States. He had experience in government because he was vice president under George Washington. His term of office was difficult because he followed George Washington as president and because he made difficult and unpopular decisions. He *negotiated* peace with both France and England. *Although* it was an unpopular decision, he is *remembered* for keeping the young country out of war at a time when the government did not have money for an army.

Thomas Jefferson is one of America's favorite heroes. He served his country well on many occasions. He wrote the Declaration of Independence. He served as secretary of state under George Washington. Later, Jefferson was the first ambassador to France. When he *returned,* he ran for president but lost.

Because he had the second highest number of votes, he became vice president. He was later elected third president of the United States. As president, he doubled the size of the country with the Louisiana Purchase from France. Jefferson's many *accomplishments earned* him a place in history.

James Madison played an important role in the development of the United States. He was the secretary of the Constitutional Convention and helped to write the Constitution. After Jefferson completed his term in office, the people elected Madison the fourth president. His term in office was very difficult. He wanted peace, but Congress wanted war with *Britain* and Spain. The British were supporting Indian *attacks* on the Americans in the West. As problems *continued,* and because the Americans wanted more *territories,* Madison *declared* war against Britain in 1812.

For other presidents, see the summary of U.S. presidents in Appendix 6.

Activity Section

Activity 1

Circle the correct response.

1. _____ was the first president of the United States.
   a. Thomas Jefferson   b. George Washington

2. _____ was the third president of the United States.
   a. Thomas Jefferson   b. James Madison

3. Washington was the _____ .
   a. commander of the army   b. first ambassador to France

4. Washington served _____ .
   a. one term   b. two terms

5. John Adams was a(n) _____ president.
   a. popular   b. unpopular

6. John Adams made _____ decisions.
   a. easy   b. difficult

7. John Adams negotiated peace with _____ .
   a. France and Spain   b. France and England

Activity 2

Write true or false after each sentence.

1. George Washington was a great leader. _____

2. Thomas Jefferson was the second president of the U.S. _____

3. Washington attended the first Continental Congress. _____

4. Jefferson was the third president of the U.S. _____

5. Madison was the secretary of the Continental Congress. _____

6. Madison was the second president of the U.S. _____

7. Madison declared war against Britain in 1812. _____

8. Jefferson wrote the Declaration of Independence. _____

Activity 3

Practice these sentences.

1. Washington **negotiated** for his country.
   > fought
   > worked

2. Washington was a **leader.**
   > commander
   > fighter
   > president

3. Jefferson served as **secretary of state.**
   > ambassador to France
   > vice president
   > president

4. Who was **the first president of the U.S.? George Washington.**

George Washington	The first president
the third president of the U.S.	Thomas Jefferson
Thomas Jefferson	The third president

Quiz

Match the two columns to complete each sentence.

1. Jefferson   _____ kept the young country out of war.

2. The nation elected Washington   _____ fought against the English and won.

3. The nation elected Jefferson   _____ declared war against Britain in 1812.

4. Washington   _____ with the Louisiana Purchase.

5. Madison   _____ the third president of the U.S.

6. The size of the U.S. doubled   _1_ wrote the Declaration of Independence.

7. Adams   _____ the first president of the U.S.

8. The Constitutional Convention was held   _____ in Pennsylvania.

Statue of George Washington at Richmond, Virginia

Lesson 19
The Civil War

Objectives

On completion of Lesson 19, students will be able to **(1)** identify the 16th president of the United States, **(2)** state the importance of the 16th president, and **(3)** identify causes of the Civil War.

The Civil War, or the War between the States, was one of the most difficult times for the United States. The war divided the country into two *enemy camps:* the Union Army, in the North, and the Confederate Army, in the South. Civil wars are destructive. They *match* brothers against brothers and friends against friends.

Many i*ssues* led to the Civil War. One of the principal causes of the war was the issue of *slavery.* Slavery in the South kept the economy of the South strong. The southern politicians and businessmen knew that if they abolished slavery, the economy of the South would fall. Another reason for the war was the right of a state to separate from the union of the United States. Another problem was the election of Abraham Lincoln as the 16th president of the United States.

Four days after Lincoln was elected, the southern states *left* the Union and *formed* the Confederate States of America. The southern soldiers, or the rebels, wore a gray-brown uniform and *marched* behind the Dixie flag. The South, led by General Robert E. Lee, fought hard to keep their way of life. They felt that the central or federal government wanted too much control over their *lives.* Many young men lost their lives during the Civil War. It destroyed the economy of the South.

The northern army was the Union Army. The soldiers, or Yankees, wore blue uniforms. Although the Yankees had more money and more soldiers, it took a long and *bloody* battle that lasted five years to defeat the South. Finally, after the death of hundreds of thousands of boys and young men on each side, the Civil War ended. The war *destroyed* the southern countryside and burned many southern cities.

Lincoln *hated* the war, but he wanted the states to be a Union under one government. He also wanted all states to obey the laws of the Constitution. He made many famous *speeches* about the Union and about liberty.

After the bloody three-day battle at Gettysburg, Lincoln gave his Gettysburg *Address*. In this speech, he *emphasized* that the United States was indivisible. After the surrender of the South, the country began rebuilding the cities and the economy destroyed by the war. Lincoln continued his work for freedom. He issued the Emancipation Proclamation, which set all slaves free. Once the war was *over* and the Union preserved, Lincoln was ready to *rebuild* and *strengthen* the country. However, only a few days after the war was over, the 16th president of the United States was *assassinated*.

See Appendix 10 for Abraham Lincoln's complete speech, "The Gettysburg Address."

Activity Section

Activity 1

Refer to the passage to complete this exercise.

The Civil War was a _____ time for the United States.

The War divided the country into two _____ camps: the

Union Army, in the North, and the _____ , in the South.

Civil wars are destructive because they match _____

against _____ and friends _____ friends.

One of the principal causes of the war was _____ . Slavery

kept the _____ of the South strong. Another reason for

the war was the _____ of a state to separate from the

_____ . Another problem was the election of

_____ as the 16th president of the U.S.

Activity 2 (pair or group work)

Match the two columns to answer each question.

1. The southern states left the Union. When?   _____ southern soldiers

2. Who were the rebels?   1 _____ when Lincoln was elected

3. What was the name for the northern soldiers?   _____ a few days after the war

4. Who wore blue uniforms?   _____ five years

5. What did Lincoln want the states to obey?   _____ hundreds of thousands

6. When was Lincoln assassinated?   _____ Yankees

7. The Civil War lasted a few years. How many?   _____ War between the States

8. How many people were killed in the Civil War?   _____ the Constitution

9. What is the Civil War also called?   _____ Lincoln

10. Who issued the Emancipation Proclamation?   _____ northern soldiers

Quiz

Circle the correct response.

1. Lincoln was the _____ of the U.S.
   a. third president   b. 16th president

2. Lincoln _____ .
   a. wrote the Constitution   b. abolished slavery

3. One of the causes of the Civil War was _____ .
   a. economic differences   b. brothers against brothers

4. The Civil War was also about _____ .
   a. control of the central government   b. control of state government

5. Lincoln wanted a _____ country.
   a. united   b. divided

Lesson 20
The Industrial Age

Objectives

On completion of Lesson 20, students will be able to **(1)** name one invention and **(2)** identify the industrial age.

The 20th *century* created great changes in America. The first change was geographic. America *spread across* to the west. It included not only the Louisiana Purchase, but also the Northern *Passage,* all the way to Oregon. The U.S. got the northern part of Mexico, which included California, Texas, Colorado, Arizona, and New Mexico, after the war with Mexico. The second change was population *movement.* Young people left small towns and farms and went to the city to look for *jobs* and new opportunities. The third change was economic. Factories created new jobs. For more than 100 years America was an agricultural society. Then, the new industrial *age* began. America changed forever.

The Yankee spirit of adventure and freedom and the belief that everyone could *get rich* led to new and *exciting* inventions. *Moreover,* the use of *coal* and *rivers* for electricity provided the power to use large machines. Inventors such as Eli Whitney, Henry Ford, and Thomas Edison changed work in America greatly. Factories *ruled* the economy using new inventions. Eli Whitney's *cotton gin* made *cloth* faster than 20 workers could. Thomas Edison invented the *light bulb,* and *factories* stayed open longer hours. Henry Ford improved the factory system when he introduced the assembly line. Everyone did one job *over and over.* In that way, they produced cars faster. *Furthermore,* they discovered that production could go faster if products looked the same. *Mass* production *entered* the industrial world. The way people worked changed forever. A great number of small shops closed. The competition from big industry was too much. There was little *room* in these new industries for artists or *craftsmen.* The *worker* was a slave to a machine that never got *tired,* never got *hungry,* and never *complained.*

Industrialization changed American society. Men and women left the farms to seek jobs in the factories. There were so many workers seeking jobs that owners paid low *wages.* There were no laws to protect workers. Since the machines could work all day, the owners wanted the workers to work long hours. Many women and children went to work for very low wages and worked in *unhealthy* conditions. Sometimes they stood long hours *without breaks* or *inhaled lint* that was dangerous to their *health.* Men, women, and children became part of a great machine, the factory.

Activity Section

Activity 1

Practice these sentences.

1. The **first** change was **geographic.**

second	population movement
third	economic
fourth	industrial

2. **George Washington Carver** was an inventor.

   Eli Whitney
   Alexander Graham Bell
   Thomas Edison

3. **Alexander Graham Bell** invented the **typewriter.**

Thomas Edison	light bulb
Eli Whitney	cotton gin
Elias Howe	sewing machine

4. Many **people** left the farms and went to the factories.

   women
   men
   children
   boys
   girls

5. **Men** left the farms to seek jobs.

   Women
   Young people
   Farmers

Activity 2

Writer <u>true</u> or <u>false</u> after each sentence.

1. The agricultural age began in the 20th century. _____

2. During the industrial revolution many people worked in unhealthy conditions. _____

3. Electricity helped machines work faster. _____

4. For more than 100 years, America was a farming society. _____

5. Americans invented machines to help the poor. _____

6. Only men worked in factories. _____

7. All workers earned a lot of money. _____

8. Industrialization did not change American society. _____

Quiz

Match the two columns to complete each sentence.

1. Eli Whitney   _____ produced cars.

2. Henry Ford   _____ invented the light bulb.

3. Thomas Edison   _____ pay per hour, week, or day.

4. Wage is   _____ great changes in America.

5. The 20th century created   _____ look the same.

6. Mass-produced articles   __1__ invented the cotton gin.

Lesson 21

World War I and World War II

Objectives

On completion of Lesson 21, students will be able to (**1**) identify two countries that fought with the United States in World War I, (**2**) identify two countries that fought with the United States in World War II, (**3**) identify what happened at Pearl Harbor, and (**4**) identify how Hiroshima was destroyed.

In 1914, Europe was at war. Germany and Austria fought against England, France, and Russia. America, under President Wilson, wanted to stay neutral. But soon German submarines *sank* American *ships,* and many people died at sea. Finally, in 1917, after the Germans sank the Lusitania and 1,000 people died, Congress declared war on Germany. America entered World War I.

America began to change its economy to a war economy. The draft, the selection of young men by lottery, began. Young men were sent, as the *song* says, "Over there . . ." to help Europe win the war. The young new soldiers, the Yanks, took new planes, money, and war supplies to the armies in Europe. With American help, the English and French finally won the war. Germany *signed* the armistice in 1918. America's role in the world changed forever.

In 1939, Germany attacked Europe again. Two armies were at war. France, England, and Russia were the Allied powers.

Germany, Italy, and Japan were the Axis powers. America was neutral. America did not want to send people to war again.

On December 7, 1941, Japan *bombed* Pearl Harbor and destroyed the American *fleet.* Congress declared war on Germany, Italy, and Japan and *joined* the Allied Forces. Soldiers fought the war on two fronts: the western front in Europe and the war in the Pacific. Americans entered the war with determination and economic power. It was a terrible war. Hundreds of thousands of men, women, and children died during this war on all sides of the world. This was really a world war—one that no one would ever *forget*. The Allied forces defeated the Axis powers in 1945. General Eisenhower was commander of those forces in Europe. General Douglas MacArthur led the forces in the Pacific against the Japanese army and navy. After a long war, the Japanese refused to *surrender*.

Early in the morning on August 6, 1945, an American bomber *dropped* the first atomic bomb on Hiroshima, Japan. This first bomb alone killed at least 70,000 people. Still the Japanese did not surrender. On August 9, American forces dropped a second bomb on Nagasaki. This new atomic bomb changed the face of the war. These two bombs left *traces* of radiation in the bodies of the *survivors* and in the earth they walked on. Japan surrendered. World War II ended.

Activity Section

Activity 1 (pair or group work)

Ask a classmate the following questions. Then write the answers.

1. Who were allies with the U.S. in World War I?

_____

2. When did America enter the war?

_____

3. What did the German submarines do?

_____

4. When did Germany sign the armistice?

_____

5. What countries fought against the U.S. in World War I?

_____

Activity 2

Circle the correct response.

1. The U.S. entered World War I in _____ .
   a. 1917   b. 1914

2. _____ declared war on Germany.
   a. Congress   b. the president

3. Germany signed the armistice in _____ .
   a. 1918   b. 1917

4. World War II began in _____ .
   a. 1939   b.1951

5. The _____ bombed Pearl Harbor.
   a. Japanese   b. Germans

Activity 3

Circle the correct response.

1. Who fought against England, France, and Russia in 1914?
   a. Germany and Austria   b. Italy and Germany   c. Italy and Austria

2. When did America declare war on Germany?
   a. in 1914   b. in 1918   c. in 1917

3. When did World War II begin?
   a. in 1939   b. in 1941   c. in 1945

4. When did the Japanese bomb Pearl Harbor?
   a. in December 1941   b. in December 1914   c. in December 1939

5. Where did the Americans drop the first atomic bomb?
   a. Hiroshima   b. Nagasaki   c. Tokyo

Quiz

Write <u>true</u> or <u>false</u> after each sentence.

1. England, France, and Russia fought on the same side in World War I. _____

2. America did not enter World War II. _____

3. France, England, Russia, and the U.S. were allies in World War II. _____

4. The Japanese bombed Pearl Harbor. _____

5. The Americans bombed Japan. _____

Statue of Marines on Iwo Jima (World War II), Arlington, Virginia

Lesson 22
The Depression

Objectives

On completion of Lesson 22, students will be able to **(1)** identify the president during the Depression and **(2)** identify one cause of the Depression.

Americans suffered greatly during the Depression of 1929. There were many reasons for the Depression. Factories produced too many products. *Tariffs* were high on *imports,* so trade between countries was difficult. New machines put people out of work. One of the big reasons for the Depression was the *Stock Market Crash.* This crash happened on Tuesday, October 29, 1929.

The Stock Market Crash *caused* many problems. Banks *closed,* and people lost their money. Factories closed, and millions of people lost their jobs. They did not have money to buy goods, so stores closed. Many people lost their homes. Many *businessmen committed* suicide. Some people died because they had no food. Others died because they had no medical attention. There were long lines of people waiting for food. These lines were called the "bread lines." Americans suffered for ten long years.

In 1932, Franklin D. Roosevelt became president. He promised to improve the life of every American. The president and Congress promised jobs for people out of work.

Congress started the WPA, the Works Progress Administration, and the PWA, the Public Works Administration. These projects *built roads,* schools, *libraries,* public offices, *bridges,* and other buildings. The government *lent* money for home *mortgages* and *insured* banks and people's savings. President Roosevelt also started the Social Security system to help people during *retirement.* Roosevelt's big plan, the New Deal, placed America on track again.

Activity Section

Activity 1

Write true or false after each sentence.

1. There was only one reason for the Depression. _____

2. The Stock Market Crash was the big reason for the Depression. _____

3. Banks closed during the Depression. _____

4. Some people died because they had no medical attention. _____

5. During the Depression everyone had food. _____

Activity 2 (pair or group work)

Read each sentence. Write a negative sentence to say what is not correct.

1. The Depression was in 1829.

   The Depression was not in 1829. _____

2. Factories were open.

   _____

3. Banks were open.

   _____

4. Trade between countries was easy.

   _____

5. The president promised money for everyone.

   _____

6. Low tariffs caused economic problems.

   _____

Activity 3

Practice these sentences.

1. **Banks** closed. People lost their **savings.**

   Factories   jobs
   Businesses   homes
   Stores   food

2. Many people lost their **jobs.**

   homes
   businesses
   friends

3. The government **started Social Security.**

   helped people
   started the Public Works Administration
   insured banks

Quiz

Answer the following questions. Use short or complete answers.

1. When did the stock market crash?

   _____

2. Who was the president during the Depression?

   _____

3. What were the "bread lines"?

   _____

4. What was the New Deal?

   _____

5. What does PWA mean?

   _____

Lesson 23
Labor Unions

Objectives

On completion of Lesson 23, students will be able to (1) identify labor unions and (2) state one reason why workers formed unions.

Workers *started* labor unions for many different reasons. There were many conflicts between labor and business. Industries brought millions of people to the cities to work in factories. Workers worked with machines that were never tired. These machines never complained *either*. Millions of immigrants came from Europe to find a new life. They worked for lower wages. There was a new class of workers. These workers worked by the hour or by the *piece*. These workers never *kept* any of the *profit*.

Workers faced many problems. A *serious* problem was that production *lines moved* too fast. It *seemed* that *owners* did not *care* about the working conditions of workers. These owners *apparently* cared only about *making money*. Many factory buildings were *unsafe*. Conditions were often unhealthy, and many people died from disease. Others died from inadequate working conditions. Wages were low, and workers had to work long hours. There were no job *guarantees* for workers. When they complained, they *lost* their jobs. There was always *someone ready* to work for *less* money.

Workers wanted rights. They formed labor unions. The first labor union, the Knights of Labor, began in 1869. The union demanded an eight-hour day and *better* working conditions. The union also demanded an end to child labor. The union *organized* some of the first *strikes* against employers. At first the union did not *succeed* because workers were *afraid* to *lose* their jobs. In 1881, Samuel Gompers started the AFL, the American Federation of Labor. It had more *success* than the Knights. The AFL *improved* conditions and wages for *skilled* workers. Later, in 1938, workers organized the Congress of Industrial Organizations, the CIO. The CIO called strikes against factories and *businesses* that had poor working conditions, longer than eight-hour days, or low wages.

The *process* of unionizing was not easy. It was difficult and *dangerous*. Many people were *hurt,* and some people died during the strikes. Employers *fired* workers that went on strike from their jobs. Workers now had a way to get some of the benefits of their labor.

Labor unions brought many benefits to the *working place,* but they also *created* many new problems. Sometimes union leaders used the union money for other *purposes*. Other times union workers paid unjust dues in order to work. Some unions didn't give jobs to workers who were not members. Although there were problems with the system, labor unions helped American workers. They also created a better and *safer* workplace.

Activity Section

Activity 1

Read each sentence. Write an affirmative sentence to say what is correct.

1. Workers didn't start labor unions.

   Workers started labor unions.

2. There weren't conflicts between labor and business.

   _____

3. Workers weren't afraid of losing their jobs.

   _____

4. Immigrants did not come from Europe.

   _____

5. Immigrants did not work for lower wages.

   _____

6. Workers didn't face many problems.

   _____

7. Workers didn't work by the hour or by the piece.

   _____

8. Owners didn't care only about making money.

   _____

Activity 2

Circle the correct response.

1. The _____ organized some of the first strikes.
   a. owners   b. unions

2. At first workers _____ afraid of losing their jobs.
   a. were   b. were not

3. A problem was that production lines moved _____ .
   a. fast   b. slowly

4. Conditions were _____ , and people died from disease.
   a. healthy   b. unhealthy

5. The first labor union was the _____ .
   a. American Federation of Labor   b. Knights of Labor

Quiz

Write _true_ or _false_ after each sentence.

1. The AFL is a union. _____

2. Unions protect workers' rights. _____

3. Machines are never tired. _____

4. There are never conflicts between labor and business. _____

5. Some workers worked by the hour or by the piece. _____

Lesson 24
Civil Rights Movements

Objectives

On completion of Lesson 24, students will be able to **(1)** name two movements that worked for equality for minorities and **(2)** identify Martin Luther King, Jr., as a great civil rights leader.

The civil rights movement began because there was *discrimination* against blacks, Mexicans, native Americans, and Asians. There was discrimination in schools, in jobs, and in housing. There was discrimination even in places where people ate or shopped. The *struggle* for civil rights was long, difficult, and dangerous. Although the Preamble states that the Constitution gives liberty and justice for all, the people in government did not always follow the Constitution. The government in many states was *brutal* against civil rights leaders and *followers*.

After World War II, Roosevelt set up the Fair Employment Practices Committee to protect people of color against discrimination. President Truman started the Committee on Civil Rights. Finally, the Supreme Court decided in 1954, in the case of Brown versus the Board of Education, that it was illegal for schools to segregate children by race. Everyone was not *happy*. Some people *reacted violently to positive* civil rights decisions. Martin Luther King, Jr., a great civil rights leader, led peaceful demonstrations for civil rights. Blacks and whites, rich and poor followed King. He had a dream for America. King's vision and civil rights actions *forced* the country to *reexamine* its laws and the Constitution. Martin Luther King, Jr., led his people on a nonviolent struggle for their rights. King was assassinated on April 4, 1968, but his dream is still *alive*.

After the Mexican-American War, the states of California, Texas, New Mexico, Colorado, and Nevada became part of the United States. Mexico and the United States signed the Treaty of Guadalupe Hidalgo. This *treaty* said that all Mexican citizens in these areas had equal rights with Americans. The treaty also *protected* their land and property. Furthermore, it protected the Spanish and Mexican culture of the people.

Many early settlers wanted the Mexicans' land. They placed high taxes on property. Many Mexicans lost their land. Other Mexicans left their homes and lands for *fear* of their life. In California, they didn't accept Mexicans as citizens. They did not have all the rights of citizens. Mexicans did not have the right to own land.

In the 1970s, the Mexican Americans demanded their rights. In Crystal City, Texas, Dr. Jose Angel Gutierrez led the first student *walk-out*. He registered Mexican Americans to vote under the Raza Unida Party. He won Salva County in an election. Many other leaders led the struggle for civil rights for Mexican Americans. The most famous leaders include: Tijerina, in Colorado; Corky Gonzales, in New Mexico; and Cesar Chavez, in California. A group of people made a plan for the Chicano movement. This movement fought for the rights of all Mexican Americans.

The civil rights movements helped minorities. Although there is still discrimination and racism, the chances to *fight back* are better. The U.S. Constitution says that all people have the right to liberty, justice, and an opportunity for *happiness*.

Activity Section

Activity 1

Circle the correct response.

1. The civil rights movement began because there was discrimination _____ .
   a. against minorities   b. against Europeans

2. The struggle for civil rights was _____ .
   a. easy   b. difficult

3. The case of Brown versus the Board of Education _____ important.
   a. was not   b. was

4. It is _____ for schools to segregate children by race.
   a. illegal   b. legal

5. Martin Luther King, Jr., was a great _____ .
   a. president   b. leader

6. King led _____ demonstrations.
   a. violent   b. peaceful

Activity 2

Write the number of the correct answer in the blank.

1. Who was Martin Luther King, Jr.?

2. What did King have for America?

3. When did Texas and California become part of the U.S.?

4. What was the Raza Unida?

5. Who are Tijerina, Gonzales, and Cesar Chavez?

6. What did Truman do for civil rights?

_____ after the Mexican-American War

_____ Mexican American leaders

_____ a dream

_____ He started the Committee on Civil Rights.

_____ a political party

___1___ a great civil rights leader

Quiz

Write _true_ or _false_ after each sentence.

1. There is discrimination in the U.S. today. _____

2. Some state governments were brutal to civil rights leaders. _____

3. The Brown versus the Board of Education case was in 1764. _____

4. Martin Luther King, Jr., was assassinated in 1968. _____

5. The Chicano movement fought for civil rights. _____

6. There is no racism today. _____

7. Discrimination in jobs is legal. _____

8. Cesar Chavez fought for civil rights. _____

Lesson 25

The U.S. in World Conflicts

Objectives

On completion of Lesson 25, students will be able to (1) identify the Korean and Vietnam Wars and (2) name one reason for U.S. involvement in world conflicts.

Since World War II, the United States has been involved in various conflicts around the world. These conflicts or wars were under the United Nations Security Council or treaty with a nation or nations.

In 1950 the communists of North Korea attacked South Korea. The United States joined the troops of the United Nations Security Council to defend South Korea. The Korean War, as it became known, lasted three years. A truce ended the fighting in 1953, and a peace-keeping force remained in Korea for many years.

The United States became involved in the Vietnam War as a member of the Southeast Asia Treaty Alliance. In 1955 the United States sent technical and economic assistance. Under President Dwight Eisenhower and President John F. Kennedy this assistance increased. In 1964 many American troops, ships, and planes were lost. The United States sent more military assistance. This increase, or escalation, was under President Lyndon B. Johnson. More than 500,000 troops were sent to Vietnam.

President Richard Nixon began bringing the American troops home. By January 1973 U.S. troops had left Vietnam. South Vietnam was defeated by North Vietnam in April of 1975.

Under various presidents the United States has sent military troops to a number of countries to defend a democratic form of government. President Lyndon B. Johnson sent troops to the Dominican Republic in 1965. In 1967 the U.S. helped Israel during the Arab-Israeli Six-Day-War. Again in 1973 the U.S. joined the United Nations in an Arab-Israeli peace-keeping force. In 1977 President Jimmy Carter was able to get the leaders of Egypt and Israel to renew their peace talks.

In the 1980s, under President Ronald Reagan, the United States became more involved in Central America. In order to stop the spread of Communism, military supplies were sent to El Salvador and economic aid was stopped to Nicaragua. U.S. troops forced the Communists off the Island of Grenada. President George Bush sent troops to Panama.

In 1990 Iraq, under the direction of Saddam Hussein, invaded Kuwait. The United Nations Security Council voted to send troops to force Iraq out of Kuwait. The United States, under President George Bush, sent thousands of troops to Saudi Arabia. This short war began in January of 1991 and ended in late February of the same year. Many nations were involved in the war. This war was known as the Persian Gulf War or Desert Storm.

Activity Section

Activity 1

Choose words from the box. Fill in the blanks to complete each sentence.

United Nations	truce
Communism	Desert Storm
Lyndon B. Johnson	January 1973
Vietnam War	United States

1. In 1953 a _____ ended the fighting in Korea.

2. The United States became involved in the _____ as a member of the Southeast Asia Treaty Alliance.

3. By _____ U.S. troops had left Vietnam.

4. In order to stop the spread of _____ , military supplies were sent to El Salvador and economic aid was stopped to Nicaragua.

5. In 1973 the U.S. joined the _____ in an Arab-Israeli peace-keeping force.

6. President _____ sent troops to the Dominican Republic in 1965.

Activity 2

Read each sentence. Write an affirmative sentence to say what is correct.

1. The United States didn't send troops to defend South Korea.

   <u>The United States sent troops to defend South Korea.</u>

2. In 1975 South Vietnam wasn't defeated by North Vietnam.

   _____

3. The United States doesn't send military troops to help other countries.

   _____

4. The United States isn't a part of the United Nations Security Council.

   _____

5. President George Bush didn't send troops to Saudi Arabia in 1990.

   _____

6. Military supplies weren't sent to El Salvador to help stop the spread of Communism.

   _____

Quiz

Write <u>true</u> or <u>false</u> after each sentence.

1. President Johnson sent more troops to Vietnam.   _____

2. In 1950 the Communists of South Korea attacked North Korea.   _____

3. The Korean War lasted three years.   _____

4. In 1967 the U.S. helped Israel during the Six-Day-War.   _____

5. In 1977 Iraq invaded Kuwait.   _____

6. President Jimmy Carter was able to get the leaders of Egypt and Israel to renew peace talks.   _____

Lesson 26
The 42nd President

Objectives
On completion of Lesson 26, students will be able to (**1**) state simple facts about the 42nd president of the U.S. and (**2**) identify some domestic and foreign problems.

The president of the United States is the head of the executive branch. The executive branch enforces the laws of the U.S. The president leads the country. The president directs the federal government. The president and his cabinet of men and women enforce federal laws.

In November of 1992, William Jefferson Clinton was elected as the 42nd president of the United States. Albert Gore (a U.S. senator from Tennessee) was elected as vice president. Clinton took office in January of 1993.

William Jefferson Clinton was born in Hope, Arkansas on August 19, 1946. He attended Georgetown University and Yale University. He became a lawyer. He served as attorney general of Arkansas from 1977–1979. He served as governor of Arkansas from 1979–1981. While serving a second term as governor of Arkansas, he was elected president of the United States.

The president is responsible for shaping both domestic and foreign policies. Domestic policies deal with things within the U.S. Foreign policies deal with things outside of the U.S. When President Clinton took office, he had to face great domestic problems within the United States.

Education and health care were important issues during President Clinton's first term. He also had to deal with crises in the Middle East and Bosnia, along with dramatic international political changes resulting from the collapse of the former Soviet Union. At home, Clinton's administration was troubled by questions over his involvement in what came to be known as the Whitewater scandal.

President Clinton's wife, First Lady Hillary Rodham Clinton, has played a prominent role in the administration.

In November 1996, Clinton was reelected to serve a second term in office. He is the first Democrat in two generations to win reelection.

Activity Section

Activity 1

Match the two columns to complete each sentence.

1. The president of the U.S. is the _____ the federal government.

2. Foreign policies deal with things _____ in 1993.

3. The president directs _____ Hope, Arkansas.

4. William Jefferson Clinton was elected _____ outside the U.S.

5. Domestic policies deal with __1__ head of the executive branch.

6. William Jefferson Clinton was born in _____ Tennessee.

7. Albert Gore was a senator from _____ the 42nd president.

8. President Clinton took office _____ within the U.S.

Activity 2

Circle the correct response.

1. William Jefferson Clinton was elected as the _____ president in November of 1992.
   a. 40th   b. 38th   c. 42nd

2. The president and his cabinet of men and women _____ the laws.
   a. enforce   b. explain   c. make

3. The president works in the _____ branch.
   a. legislative   b. executive   c. judicial

4. The next presidential election is in _____ .
   a. 1999   b. 2000   c. 2002

5. William Jefferson Clinton was both governor and _____ of Arkansas.
   a. secretary   b. treasurer   c. attorney general

Quiz

Answer the following questions.

1. Who is the 42nd president of the United States?

   _____

2. What do foreign policies deal with?

   _____

3. What state was William Jefferson Clinton governor of?

   _____

4. What do domestic policies deal with?

   _____

5. Who is Albert Gore?

   _____

Lesson 27
Holidays

Objectives

On completion of Lesson 27, students will be able to (**1**) name three national holidays, (**2**) identify Presidents' Day, and (**3**) identify July 4 as Independence Day.

America celebrates many *holidays*. Some are federal holidays. Others are not. On many of these days, government offices may close. Offices like the INS, the Post Office, City Hall, and county offices may close. On some holidays, many *stores* and places of business may close also. *Besides* a day off from work or school, holidays remind us of important *events* in *our* history.

Independence Day

On every July 4, Americans celebrate the day in 1776 when they became independent from England. There are usually many *parades* and *fireworks* to celebrate this day.

Columbus Day

Christopher Columbus discovered America. Most of the countries in the Americas celebrate the discovery of America on October 12. Many cities, especially where there are Italians, have a Columbus Day parade.

Memorial Day

Every year on May 30, Americans *honor* the men who fought and died to keep Americans free. There are parades and special *services* in *cemeteries* to honor our heroes.

Thanksgiving Day

On the last Thursday of November, families get together to celebrate this day. Many families have a *meal* with *turkey* on Thanksgiving Day. America remembers that the Pilgrims and the native Americans celebrated the first Thanksgiving together. The Pilgrims *thanked* the native Americans. They helped the Pilgrims survive the first winter.

Lincoln's Birthday

Americans remember Abraham Lincoln, the 16th president of the United States, on February 12. Lincoln *freed* the slaves and *saved* the union.

Washington's Birthday

On February 22 Americans remember George Washington. He led many important battles during the Revolutionary War and was the first president of the United States. Presidents' Day celebrates both Lincoln's and Washington's birthdays.

Labor Day

On the first Monday of September, workers have a day off from work. Many families *go on picnics* on Labor Day. They eat *hot dogs, hamburgers,* and *potato salad.*

Some people play baseball or other games. For school children, Labor Day is usually the last day of summer vacation before school starts again.

Activity Section

Activity 1 (pair or group work)

Match the two columns to complete each sentence.

1. July 4 is

2. On Thanksgiving Day

3. October 12 celebrates

4. Presidents' Day celebrates

5. Memorial Day remembers the

_____ many families eat turkey.

_____ Columbus Day.

_____ Lincoln and Washington.

_____ people who fought and died for America.

__1__ Independence Day.

Activity 2

Answer the following questions. Use short or complete answers.

1. Who discovered America?

_____

2. When does the U.S. celebrate Columbus Day?

_____

3. When is Thanksgiving Day?

_____

4. When is Labor Day?

_____

5. When do federal offices close?

_____

Activity 3 (pair work)

Read each sentence. Write an affirmative sentence to say what is correct.

1. America doesn't celebrate many holidays.

   America celebrates many holidays.
   _____

2. Government offices don't close on federal holidays.

   _____

3. Federal *employees* don't get a day off on federal holidays.

   _____

4. Holidays don't remind us of events in our history.

   _____

5. The fourth of July isn't Independence Day.

   _____

6. Thanksgiving Day isn't the last Thursday in November.

   _____

Quiz

Write <u>true</u> or <u>false</u> after each sentence.

1. The U.S. became independent on July 4, 1776. _____

2. Labor Day, Memorial Day, and Sundays are three national holidays. _____

3. The last Thursday in November is Memorial Day. _____

4. Christopher Columbus discovered Italy. _____

5. The INS, the Post Office, and City Hall are businesses. _____

Lesson 28
The American Flag

Objectives

On completion of Lesson 28, students will be able to **(1)** identify and describe the United States flag, **(2)** state the number of stars and stripes, and **(3)** identify "The Star-Spangled Banner."

Every country in the world chooses a flag. The flag is a symbol of the country. Usually citizens of a country are proud of their flag. Most flags represent certain values of the country. The U.S. flag has *stars* and *stripes*. The U.S. flag has three colors. The three *colors* are red, white, and blue. The red *represents courage;* the white represents *truth;* and the blue represents *justice*. The flag has 13 stripes. There are seven red stripes and six white stripes. The 13 stripes represent the 13 original colonies of the United States. The flag also has a blue *square* with white stars. Each star represents a state of the Union. There are now 50 stars in the blue square, because Hawaii and Alaska are the 49th and 50th states. Each state also has its own flag. Each state chooses symbols and colors that represent the state.

Every country also has a national *anthem*. An anthem is a hymn of *allegiance*. The national anthem of the U.S. is "The Star-Spangled Banner." People *sing* "The Star-Spangled Banner" at official functions. People also sing or *play* the anthem at certain sports events. Francis Scott Key wrote "The Star-Spangled Banner." It begins with the

U.S. flag today

U.S. flag in 1776

words "Oh say can you see, by the *dawn's* early *light.*"

See Appendix 9 for the words to "The Star-Spangled Banner."

Activity Section

Activity 1

Complete each sentence with the correct information.

1. The colors of the U.S. flag are _____ .

2. The U.S. flag has _____ stripes.

3. The U.S. flag has 50 _____ .

4. There are _____ red stripes on the U.S. flag.

5. Each white star represents _____ .

6. The first line of the national anthem says _____

_____ .

7. The stripes on the U.S. flag represent the original _____ .

Activity 2

Circle the correct answer to each question.

1. Do the states have flags?
   a. Yes, they do.   b. No, they don't.

2. How many colors does the U.S. flag have?
   a. three   b. five

3. What is the color of the square on the flag?
   a. white   b. blue

4. What is the name of the U.S. national anthem?
   a. "America the Beautiful"   b. "The Star-Spangled Banner"

5. What is an anthem?
   a. a hymn   b. a poem

6. What are the first few words of "The Star-Spangled Banner"?
   a. "Oh beautiful . . . "   b. "Oh say can you see . . . "

Activity 3

Practice these sentences.

1. Every country has **a flag.**

> a national anthem
> symbols
> values

2. People play "The Star-Spangled Banner" at **official functions.**

> special events
> sport events
> the Olympics

3. The flag has **three colors.**

> 13 stripes
> 50 stars
> a blue square

4. The **flag** represents **the U.S.**

red	courage
white	truth
blue	justice

Quiz

Match the two columns to complete each sentence.

1. The flag is a symbol   _____ 13 stripes.

2. The U.S. flag has   _____ "The Star-Spangled Banner."

3. The national anthem is   _____ hymn of allegiance.

4. An anthem is a   _____ 50 stars on the U.S. flag.

5. There are   _____ of the country.

Lesson 29
The Statue of Liberty

Objectives

On completion of Lesson 29, students will be able to **(1)** identify the Statue of Liberty and **(2)** identify what it stands for.

The Statue of Liberty was a *gift* from the people of France. It welcomes people from *all over* the world. France gave the Statue of Liberty to the United States in 1886. To many people, the Statue of Liberty is also a symbol of international *friendship*. Some immigrants *anxiously* await their arrival to New York *harbor*. They know Lady Liberty will *greet* them there.

The Statue of Liberty stands with her arm stretched *upward*. She holds a *torch* to greet immigrants night and day as they enter the United States. The statue is on Liberty Island in the New York harbor. The immigration processing offices on Ellis Island are *across* from the statue. Thousands of immigrants came through the doors of the offices of Ellis Island. To many of these immigrants, Lady Liberty, the statue, is a symbol of a better *future*. To some, it is a symbol of freedom. To others, it is a symbol of opportunity. Today there is a museum on Ellis Island. This museum shows *exhibits* of the different people that came to America. After 100 years, the *sea, sun,* and *wind* damaged the statue. For her 100th anniversary, Americans from all over the country *donated* money to make her beautiful again. When the workers completed the job, Americans had a special 100-year birthday party for Lady Liberty.

Lady Liberty's 100-year celebration was special. Many thousands of tourists visited Ellis Island to see the Statue of Liberty. Many people decorated their boats and ships with lights and the colors of the American flag. A large number of these boats had a parade around New York Harbor for the occasion. Americans are very proud that Lady Liberty is beautiful again.

Activity Section

Activity 1 (pair or group work)

Read each sentence. Write an affirmative sentence to say what is correct.

1. The Statue of Liberty wasn't a gift from France.

   The Statue of Liberty was a gift from France.

2. France didn't give the Statue of Liberty in 1886.

   _____

3. The statue isn't a symbol of a better future to many people.

   _____

4. There isn't a museum on Ellis Island.

   _____

5. The Statue of Liberty doesn't hold a torch.

   _____

Activity 2

Circle the correct response.

1. Liberty Island is in _____ .
   a. New York   b. the Caribbean

2. The Statue of Liberty welcomes _____ .
   a. Americans   b. all people

3. The Statue of Liberty greets immigrants _____ .
   a. by night   b. by day and night

4. Lady Liberty was 100 years old _____ .
   a. in 1987   b. in 1986

5. Many immigrants enter the country through _____ .
   a. Manhattan Island   b. Ellis Island

Quiz

Answer the following questions. Use short or complete answers.

1. What country gave the Statue of Liberty to the U.S.?

_____

2. What is another name for the Statue of Liberty?

_____

3. What does the Statue of Liberty stand for?

_____

4. Where is Ellis Island?

_____

5. What does Lady Liberty have in her hand?

_____

Lesson 30
The Pledge of Allegiance

Objectives

On completion of Lesson 30, students will be able to (1) say the Pledge of Allegiance, (2) identify the Pledge of Allegiance as a promise, and (3) identify the U.S. as a republic.

I pledge allegiance to the flag of the United States of America and to the republic for which it stands, one nation under God, indivisible, with liberty and justice for all.

People of all nations promise to be *loyal* to their country. Americans promise loyalty to the U.S. every time they say the Pledge of *Allegiance*. A pledge is a *promise* that people make to America. *Out of respect* for the flag that represents their country, citizens *stand* and place their right hands over their *hearts while* they say the Pledge of Allegiance.

Americans are proud of their form of government. In the Pledge of Allegiance, Americans say that their country is the United States of America. It is a union of many states. It is not a federation of states. It is one nation. Furthermore, citizens say their country is a republic. This means that the government is by the people and for the people. It also means that Americans choose a democratic form of government. This decision gives them the opportunity to vote for candidates at all levels of government.

The Pledge of Allegiance says that our Union is *indivisible,* which means it cannot be separated. When the southern states tried to separate from the Union, America fought the Civil War. The Pledge of Allegiance also promises that this country is "under God." Many people came to America for religious freedom. They believed that people have the right to religious freedom. The U.S. does not have an official religion. Americans believe that an official religion would conflict with religious freedom. The last phrase of the Pledge of Allegiance—with liberty and justice for all—is one reason millions of immigrants came to America. They wanted liberty and justice. The fight for liberty and justice for everyone continues even today. Americans pledge allegiance to the flag. They pledge liberty and justice for all. It is everyone's responsibility to make these promises true.

Activity Section

Activity 1

Read each sentence. Write an affirmative sentence to say what is correct.

1. The Pledge of Allegiance is not a promise.

   The Pledge of Allegiance is a promise.

2. Americans do not pledge allegiance to the flag.

   _____

3. The United States is not one nation.

   _____

4. Liberty and justice are not for all.

   _____

5. Americans are not proud of their form of government.

   _____

6. The United States is not a republic.

   _____

7. In the U.S., government is not by the people and for the people.

   _____

8. Americans don't have a democratic form of government.

   _____

Activity 2

Write the number of the correct answer in the blank.

1. What is a pledge?   _____ No, it is not.

2. To what do we pledge allegiance?   _____ No, there is not.

3. Is the U.S. a federation of states?   _____ "...with liberty and justice for all."

4. Is there an official religion in the U.S.?   _____ "I pledge allegiance to the flag..."

5. What is the last line of the Pledge   _____ to the flag.
   of Allegiance?

6. How does the Pledge of Allegiance   _____ It's a promise.
   begin?

Quiz

Write <u>true</u> or <u>false</u> after each sentence.

1. People place their right hands over their hearts to say the Pledge of Allegiance. _____

2. The Pledge of Allegiance is a Promise. _____

3. The U.S. has a republican form of government. _____

4. The U.S. is many nations. _____

5. The fight for liberty and justice is over. _____

6. The Pledge of Allegiance says the U.S. is not indivisible. _____

Lesson 31
The Capital

Objectives
On completion of Lesson 31, students will be able to (1) identify and locate the capital of the United States on a map and (2) indicate the location of the White House.

Washington, D.C. (District of Columbia), is the capital of the United States. It is there that the federal government has many of its offices.

Washington, D.C., does not belong to any state. It is not a state; it is a district. It is between the states of Maryland and Virginia. It covers only 67 *square miles*. The streets look like *spokes* of a wheel. They divide the city into four different geographic areas. Look at the map of the U.S. in the Appendix. Find Washington, D.C.

There are many government buildings in Washington, D.C. The Senate and the House of Representatives meet in the Capitol to make laws. The Supreme Court meets in the Supreme Court Building to explain laws and hear court cases. The president lives in the White House on Pennsylvania Avenue.

The center of the capital has many beautiful monuments. It has the Washington Monument, the Jefferson Memorial, the Lincoln Memorial, and many others to

remind us of our heroes. Japan *gave* the city beautiful cherry trees that *bloom* in the spring. These trees add to the beauty of the city.

Each state has a capital city. It is the city where state laws are made and where the governor directs state business.

See Appendix 2 for the names of state capitals. The names are listed under the name of the states. A star shows the location of the state capitals on the map. Learn the name of your state capital.

Activity Section

Activity 1 (pair work)

Practice the dialogue with another student.

S-1:   What is Washington, D.C.?

S-2:   It is the capital of the U.S.

S-1:   What does D.C. mean?

S-2:   It means District of Columbia.

S-1:   Is it a part of Maryland?

S-2:   No. It doesn't belong to any state.

Activity 2

Read each sentence. Write an affirmative sentence to say what is correct.

1. Washington, D.C., is not between Maryland and Virginia.

_____

2. Washington, D.C., does not cover 67 square miles.

_____

3. The Senate and the House do not meet in the Capitol.

_____

4. The Supreme Court does not explain laws.

_____

5. The White House is not on Pennsylvania Avenue.

_____

6. Washington, D.C., does not have many monuments.

_____

7. There isn't a Washington Monument in Washington, D.C.

_____

Activity 3

Circle the correct response.

1. The capital of the U.S. is between _____ .
   a. Maryland and Virginia   b. Arizona and Washington

2. The capital of the U.S. is a _____ .
   a. state   b. district

3. The city of Washington, D.C., is _____ .
   a. very big   b. very small

4. Washington, D.C., has _____ monuments.
   a. many   b. few

5. Japan gave the city _____ .
   a. a monument   b. cherry trees

Quiz

Answer the following questions. Use short or complete answers.

1. Who lives at the White House?

   _____

2. How big is the District of Columbia?

   _____

3. The White House is on an avenue. Which avenue?

   _____

4. Washington, D.C., is near Virginia. What other state is it near?

   _____

5. Where does the Supreme Court meet?

   _____

Lesson 32
State Government

Objectives

On completion of Lesson 32, students will be able to **(1)** identify three levels of government, **(2)** recognize the branches of state government, and **(3)** name the head of the state executive branch.

Government is the administration and control of public policy. In the U.S., there is a federal government and there are state and local governments.

The federal government is the largest body of government. It *plans* and *does* business for the *entire* country. The Constitution *states* the responsibility and *structure* of the federal government. Any power that the Constitution does not give to the federal government belongs to the states. The federal government is larger now than in 1787, but the *basic* laws of government are the same. The structure of government is the same. The branches of government are still the executive, the legislative, and the judicial branches. Each branch has *specific* functions.

In 1787, the United states had only 13 states. Today there are 50 states in the U.S. The founding fathers *planned* for more states to join the Union. They wanted the new states to have the same type of government as the original states.

Every state government has a constitution. That constitution cannot disagree with the Constitution of the United States. Every state government also has three branches of government: the executive, the legislative, and the judicial.

Laws *passed* by states cannot disagree with the federal Constitution. In addition, state laws apply only to the people that live in the state. Every state has the responsibility to protect the lives of the people in that state. The state is responsible for transportation, education, and the laws of business in that state. The federal and state governments work together in many areas. Housing and health care are two of those areas.

The head of the state executive branch is the governor. The governor directs the state government. Forty-three states have a lieutenant governor as the second in command. Other state officers usually include secretary of state, state treasurer, and attorney general. A cabinet is appointed to help the governor.

All states except Nebraska have a two-house legislature to make state laws. Each state constitution gives the number in the state Senate and in their state House of Representatives (also called the Assembly). The state legislative branch makes the state laws.

The state judicial branch has a state Supreme Court and courts of appeal at the state level. The main trial courts are at the county and city levels. They are called Superior Court, District Court, and municipal or city courts. The state judicial branch explains and interprets the state laws.

See Appendix 5 for the structure of state governments.

Activity Section

Activity 1

Complete each sentence with the correct information.

1. In the United States there is a federal government and there are _____ and local governments.

2. There are _____ states in the United States.

3. The _____ is the head of the state executive branch.

4. Every state government has a state _____ .

5. The state judicial branch has a state _____ Court.

6. The state legislative branch _____ the state laws.

7. Laws passed by states _____ disagree with the federal Constitution.

8. A _____ is appointed to help the governor.

Activity 2

Circle the correct response.

1. There are _____ levels of government in the U.S.
   a. four   b. two   c. three

2. State government has _____ branches.
   a. two   b. three   c. four

3. The governor is the head of the state _____ branch.
   a. judicial   b. legislative   c. executive

4. The main trial courts are at the _____ and city levels.
   a. county   b. federal   c. state

Quiz

Write true or false after each sentence.

1. Every state has three branches of government. _____

2. State laws apply only to the people in their state. _____

3. The head of the state executive branch is the state attorney general. _____

4. All states except California have a two-house state legislature. _____

5. The state legislative branch makes state laws. _____

Lesson 33
Local Government

Objectives

On completion of Lesson 33, students will be able to (1) identify counties and cities as subdivisions of states and (2) name the heads of the county and city executive branch.

States have subdivisions, or smaller areas of local government. Local government includes county, township, municipalities, school district, and special districts. All states except Connecticut and Rhode Island have counties. New England and north central states also have townships.

Counties are subdivisions of states. Counties have charters (a plan of government). These charters indicate how the county government should run. They also indicate what officials people may elect to run the county government. A county charter cannot disagree with its state constitution or the federal Constitution. The city where county government does its business is called the county seat. County government runs programs at the local level. State and county government work together in many areas, like transportation, safety, health, and welfare.

The legislative branch of county government is an elected board of supervisors or commissioners. They make county laws. The executive branch of county government is usually also the board of supervisors or commissioners. They share their executive powers with other elected officials, such as the sheriff, a clerk, a treasurer, and a superintendent of county schools.

The county judicial branch is usually responsible for all courts in a county or township. County courts are the main trial courts and take care of major cases, such as criminal, divorce, and cases involving large sums of money. Judges are often appointed by the governor and then elected by the people at the next election.

The smallest subdivision of government is city or municipal government. There are usually many cities in a county. Cities apply to their state for permission to form a city government. The state gives the city its plan of government. A city has a city legislative branch made up of the mayor and a city council or commission.

The city executive branch includes the mayor and other elected officers such as a city clerk or city treasurer. Many cities have a hired city manager or administrator. The city executive branch is responsible for its police, fire department, city and street maintenance, and park departments.

The judicial branches of cities are under county or township government. The city (municipal or justice) courts take care of lesser cases, including traffic and small claims.

States give some money from taxes to cities. Cities also collect taxes from local people. These taxes pay for city administration, police, fire departments, parks, and other services. City government is the closest form of government to the people. People have a more immediate voice in city government because city halls are usually close to where they live. City hall is the place where city business is conducted.

School districts and special districts, such as the water district, gas and electric district, or airport districts are usually under county regulations.

Activity Section

Activity 1

Ask a classmate the following questions. Then write the answer.

1. Who is the head of the city executive branch?

_____

2. What is the smallest subdivision of government?

_____

3. Which states don't have counties?

_____

4. What are counties and cities subdivisions of?

_____

5. Who is the head of the county executive branch?

_____

6. Who gives cities their plan of government?

_____

7. Name two things city taxes help pay for.

_____

8. Where is city business conducted?

_____

Activity 2

Match the two columns to complete each sentence.

1. Counties are subdivisions

2. The smallest subdivision of government is

3. The city executive branch is responsible for the

4. Cities also collect taxes

5. City government is the closest form of government

_____ city police and city fire
     departments.

_____ from local people.

_____city or municipal government.

_____ to the people.

_____ of states.

Quiz

Circle the correct response.

1. Counties have _____ to indicate how the county government should run.
   a. constitutions   b. charters

2. _____ government is the closest form of government to the people.
   a. city or municipal   b. state

3. Counties are subdivisions of _____ .
   a. states   b. cities

4. The board of supervisors or commissioners is usually head of both the legislative and executive branch in _____ government.
   a. state   b. county

5. The _____ and other elected officers are the head of the city executive branch.
   a. board of supervisors   b. mayor

Lesson 34
Legal Aliens

Objectives

On completion of Lesson 34, students will be able to (1) identify different types of legal aliens, (2) state what is required of legal aliens, and (3) identify felonies and misdemeanors.

There are several groups of legal aliens in the United States. First: Those immigrants who entered the United States legally and were given permanent resident status. They have been immigrated into the United States by a U.S. citizen and have passports from their own countries and legal status in the United States.

Second: Those immigrants who applied for a change of status under the Amnesty program. These immigrants who do not have permanent status must change their temporary status to permanent status. The Immigration Act of 1990 extended the time limit for changing status by one year from their original 30-month deadline. Temporary residents who are eligible legal aliens need to learn about U.S. history and government and demonstrate a minimal understanding of ordinary English. They may attend classes or take a test to show their competency in these areas. They may show they are "satisfactorily pursuing" a course of study. Some agricultural temporary workers can go ahead and apply for permanent status. They must submit an I-90 form, three photos, and have an interview with the Immigration and Naturalization Service (INS).

Third: Those immigrants who are in the United States as visitors, students, or on temporary business in the U.S. and will be returning to their own country.

The first and second group may work in the United States and must have work permits or authorized employment cards and a Social Security card. They must not apply for certain types of welfare, particularly cash assistance. Some aliens may receive a public charge waiver when they apply. If they do so, they must prove they did not receive any benefits illegally. After obtaining resident alien status, legal aliens who apply for government assistance, such as SSI, are now required to become U.S. citizens.

Legal aliens must respect the laws of the U.S. if they want to live in this country. If a legal alien commits a felony, the INS may not give him or her citizenship. A felony is a major crime such as murder, burglary, or rape. Legal aliens must not be arrested for more than three misdemeanors. A misdemeanor is an offense less serious than a felony such as shoplifting or jaywalking.

Legal aliens who obey the laws of the United States have a better chance at becoming U.S. citizens.

Activity Section

Activity 1

Refer to the text to complete this exercise.

The first and second group may _____ in the United States and

must have _____ or authorized employment cards and a

_____ . They must not apply for certain types of

_____ , particularly _____ assistance.

Some aliens may receive a _____ waiver when they apply.

If they do so, they must prove they did not receive any _____ illegally.

Activity 2 (pair work)

Practice these sentences out loud.

1. Temporary residents who are eligible legal aliens need **work permits.**

                                             a social security card.
                                             proof of birth

2. **A felony** is a major crime.
   Burglary
   Murder
   Rape

3. Temporary residents who are eligible legal aliens need to learn **United States history.**

                                             United States government
                                             ordinary English
                                             to sign their name in English

Quiz

Answer <u>true</u> or <u>false</u> after each sentence.

1. Some legal aliens have been immigrated into the U.S. by a U.S. citizen. _____

2. Temporary residents who are eligible legal aliens need to learn United States history, government, and ordinary English. _____

3. Legal aliens don't need work permits. _____

4. Eligible legal aliens who do not have permanent status must change their temporary status to permanent status. _____

5. Legal aliens can receive welfare cash assistance. _____

Lesson 35

On Becoming a Citizen

Objectives

On completion of Lesson 35, students will be able to (1) state the basic requirements to become a U.S. citizen and (2) identify required documents for citizenship.

After five years of legal permanent residency, a person who is at least 18 years old can apply for naturalization. You may become a citizen if any of the following apply to you:

- You have been a legal permanent resident for five years.
- You have been a legal permanent resident for three years, have been married to a United States citizen for those three years, and continue to be married to that U.S. citizen.
- You are the legal permanent resident child of United States citizen parents.
- You have qualifying military service.

To become a citizen, you must do the following:

- Learn to speak, read, and write English
- Learn to sign your name
- Learn some U.S. history and government
- Live in the United States, in one state, for six months continuously before you apply
- Be of good moral character
- Be loyal to the United States

The process to become a citizen is as follows:

1. File an application—INS form N400.
2. Pass an interview/examination.
3. Attend a swearing-in ceremony.

The INS authorized a few organizations to provide Section 312 standardized citizenship tests. There are local community organizations and schools where the tests are offered. The standardized test includes 20 multiple-choice questions and requires writing a few simple sentences in English. Applicants will need about 30 minutes to complete the test, which may be repeated as often as necessary. Applications are available at any immigration office. Applicants must do the following:

1. Fill out the application truthfully.
2. Pay a $95 fee in the exact amount. (This fee cannot be refunded.)
3. Fill out a fingerprint chart.
4. Include two color photographs taken within 30 days of the application.

Police stations, sheriff's offices, and other qualified persons take fingerprints. You must sign the chart in the presence of the person taking your fingerprints. Do not bend, fold, or crease the fingerprint chart.

The Immigration and Naturalization Service (INS) also requires proof of identification and other important documents, when indicated, such as the following:
- Alien registration card and receipt
- Passport
- Marriage certificate and children's birth certificates
- Any record of driving tickets

The INS reviews the application and the documents. If all the information is correct and complete, the INS sets a date for an interview. The INS officer asks the applicants about the information on their applications. Applicants must be able to sign their names. People who are over 50 years old, and who have been legal permanent residents for 20 years or more, do not have to take the exam in English. Applicants who are 55 or older, and who have been legal permanent residents for at least 15 years, do not have to take the exam in English. In either of those cases, applicants may take the examination in a language of their choice.

After the examination, the INS official files the petition for naturalization. The applicants are reviewed and investigated again. If they meet all the requirements, they will be notified to go to the final case hearing. The INS judge sets a date for the swearing-in ceremony. At this ceremony, every new citizen takes the oath of allegiance to the United States. In the oath, the applicants promise to be loyal to the United States. They give up their allegiance to their country and swear to defend the United States. At the end of the ceremony, the judge tells the applicants that they are now U.S. citizens. As U.S. citizens, they have the rights and privileges of any other American citizen. Each new citizen receives a certificate of naturalization.

Citizens have the right to vote and run for office. Naturalized citizens can run for any office, except president and vice president. If they want a job on certain federal projects, they must get a security clearance. They can enter and leave the United States at any time. They travel with an American passport. More important for many naturalized citizens is the fact that they may help other immediate members of their families to migrate to the United States.

For more information, you can call the INS toll-free at 1-800-755-0777. To request forms, you can reach the INS toll-free at 1-800-870-3676.

Activity Section

Activity 1

Circle the correct response.

1. Applicants _____ the oath of allegiance on the day that they become U.S. citizens.

   a. take   b. do not take

2. Applicants must fill out their application with _____ .

   a. false information   b. the truth

3. Applicants for citizenship _____ a fingerprint chart.

   a. do not need   b. need

4. Each new citizen receives a _____ of naturalization.

   a. certificate   b. application

5. Permanent residents _____ the right to vote.

   a. have   b. do not have

Activity 2

Match the two columns to complete each sentence.

1. Be of good   _____ the United States.

2. Fill out the application   _____ chart.

3. Pay $95   _____ unsigned photographs.

4. Include a fingerprint   _____ moral character.

5. Include two   _____ fee.

6. Be loyal to   _____ truthfully.

Activity 3

Read each sentence. Write an affirmative sentence to say what is correct.

1. Naturalized citizens cannot be senators.

   _____

2. There is not a test for applicants for citizenship.

   _____

3. New citizens do not swear to be loyal and to defend the U.S.

   _____

4. Applicants for citizenship under 50 years old who have not lived in the U.S. for 20 years do not take a literacy test.

   _____

Quiz

Write true or false after each sentence.

1. Applicants must be at least 18 years old to apply for citizenship. _____

2. Applicants must be of good moral character to apply for citizenship. _____

3. After three years of permanent residency, any resident can apply to become a citizen. _____

4. Residents can get an application at any INS office. _____

5. INS means International Service. _____

Lesson 36
Rights and Responsibilities

Objectives
On completion of Lesson 36, students will be able to (1) name a responsibility that everyone has and (2) name a right that only citizens have.

In order to protect the people of the United States, the federal government has set up certain laws. Both citizens and temporary/permanent aliens have the responsibility to obey these laws. They also have certain rights.

All persons have the obligation to respect the rights of others—their property, privacy, dignity, opinions, and religious beliefs. Each individual has the responsibility to obey and support the laws of the United States.

Workers must pay taxes and file Income Tax Reports. They must also have Social Security cards. Drivers must have a driver's license and car insurance and obey the traffic laws. Most professions require some type of license or certificate in order to work— doctors, nurses, nurses' assistants, pharmacists, and medical technicians require state licenses; teachers must be certified; building contractors and businesses require licenses or permits; so do stores and restaurants. Some of these licenses or permits are state or local. Dog owners need to get a dog license if they live in the city. Food handlers must have certain health certificates or permits.

There are some rights and responsibilities that only citizens have. Only citizens of the United States have the right to vote. When they register to vote, they have the right to choose which political party they wish to join. The two major political parties in the United States are the Democratic party and the Republican party. Then the registered citizen has the right to vote. They also have the right to run for public office.

Only citizens have the right to hold certain jobs in government offices or with federal defense contractors. Only citizens may serve on a jury. Citizens may get a U.S. passport and have the protection of the U.S. when traveling or working in a foreign country.

Everyone has the responsibility to be aware of what is happening in government and to express his or her concern to the legislators or elected leaders. Everyone should give the leaders support when needed. All are a part of government "by the people." People can start state or local laws by an initiative. They can stop a law by a referendum and remove unwanted officials by a recall. People can effectively participate in government.

Activity Section

Activity 1

Circle the correct response.

1. People can start a state or local law by a(n) _____ .
   a. recall   b. initiative

2. People can stop a state law by a(n) _____
   a. referendum   b. initiative

3. Unwanted officials can be removed by a(n) _____ .
   a. recall   b. election

4. Most professions require some type of _____ .
   a. license   b. vote

5. Citizens have to _____ before they can vote.
   a. work   b. register

Activity 2

Fill in the blanks.

1. Each individual has the responsibility to _____ and support the laws of the U.S.

2. Food handlers must have certain _____ certificates or permits.

3. Only _____ of the United states have a right to vote.

4. People can effectively participate in _____ .

5. Citizens may get a U.S. passport and have the protection of the _____ when traveling or working in a foreign country.

Quiz

Match the two columns to complete each sentence.

1. Both citizens and temporary/permanent aliens have the responsibility to

2. Only citizens of the United States

3. People can start state or local laws

4. Workers must have a

5. The two major political parties in the U.S. are the

6. Only citizens may serve

7. People can stop a law

8. Most professions require some type of license or certificate

9. Workers must pay taxes and file

10. People can remove unwanted officials

_____ Social Security card.

_____ by recall.

_____ income tax reports.

_____ on a jury.

_____ in order to work.

_____ by an initiative.

_____ obey U.S. laws.

_____ have the right to vote.

_____ by a referendum.

_____ Democratic party and the Republican party.

Appendices

Appendix 1
Map of the World

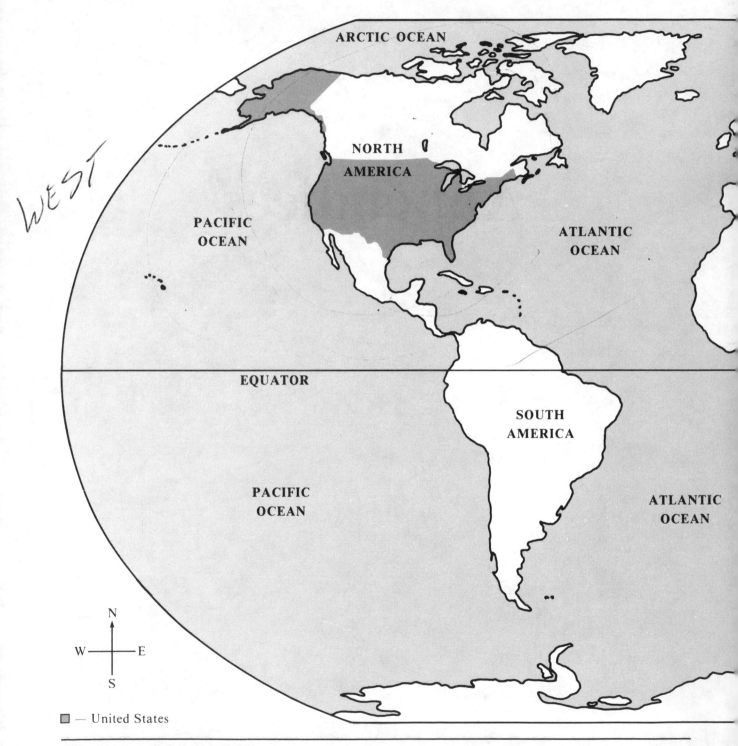

WEST

ARCTIC OCEAN

NORTH AMERICA

PACIFIC OCEAN

ATLANTIC OCEAN

EQUATOR

SOUTH AMERICA

PACIFIC OCEAN

ATLANTIC OCEAN

N
W — E
S

☐ — United States

NORTHPOLE

ARCTIC OCEAN

EUROPE

EAST

ASIA

PACIFIC
OCEAN

AFRICA

EQUATOR

INDIAN
OCEAN

AUSTRALIA

ANTARCTICA

SOUTH POLE

Appendix 2
Map of the United States

Map Key: States and Capitals

AK—Alaska
Juneau

AL—Alabama
Montgomery

AR—Arkansas
Little Rock

AZ—Arizona
Phoenix

CA—California
Sacramento

CO—Colorado
Denver

CT—Connecticut
Hartford

DE—Delaware
Dover

FL—Florida
Tallahassee

GA—Georgia
Atlanta

HI—Hawaii
Honolulu

IA—Iowa
Des Moines

ID—Idaho
Boise

IL—Illinois
Springfield

IN—Indiana
Indianapolis

KS—Kansas
Topeka

KY—Kentucky
Frankfort

LA—Louisiana
Baton Rouge

MA—Massachusetts
Boston

MD—Maryland
Annapolis

ME—Maine
Augusta

MI—Michigan
Lansing

MN—Minnesota
St. Paul

MO—Missouri
Jefferson City

MS—Mississippi
Jackson

MT—Montana
Helena

NC—North Carolina
Raleigh

ND—North Dakota
Bismarck

NE—Nebraska
Lincoln

NH—New Hampshire
Concord

NJ—New Jersey
Trenton

NM—New Mexico
Santa Fe

NV—Nevada
Carson City

NY—New York
Albany

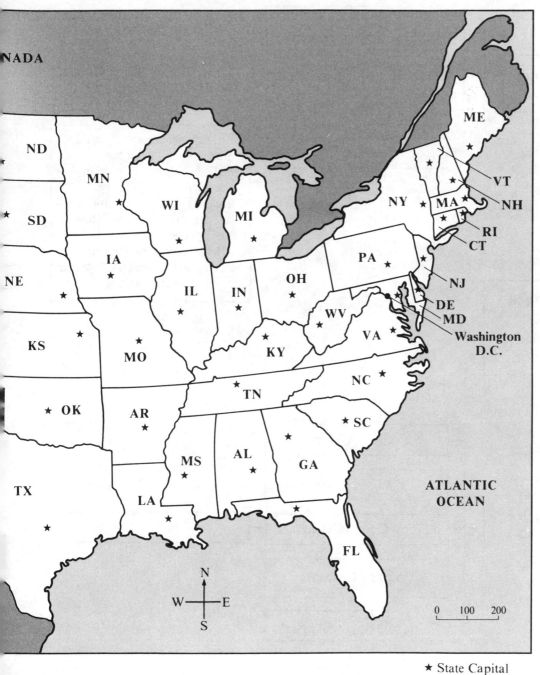

NADA

ME

ND

MN

VT

WI

MI

NY

MA

NH

SD

RI

CT

IA

PA

NE

OH

NJ

IL

IN

DE

KS

WV

MD

MO

VA

Washington D.C.

KY

NC

TN

OK

AR

SC

MS

AL

GA

TX

LA

ATLANTIC OCEAN

FL

N
W—E
S

0   100   200

OH—Ohio
      Columbus

OK—Oklahoma
      Oklahoma City

OR—Oregon
      Salem

PA—Pennsylvania
      Harrisburg

RI —Rhode Island
      Providence

SC—South Carolina
      Columbia

SD—South Dakota
      Pierre

TN—Tennessee
      Nashville

TX—Texas
      Austin

UT—Utah
      Salt Lake City

VA —Virginia
      Richmond

VT —Vermont
      Montpelier

WA—Washington
      Olympia

WI —Wisconsin
      Madison

WV—West Virginia
      Charleston

WY—Wyoming
      Cheyenne

★ State Capital

Appendix 3
Structure of the U.S. Government

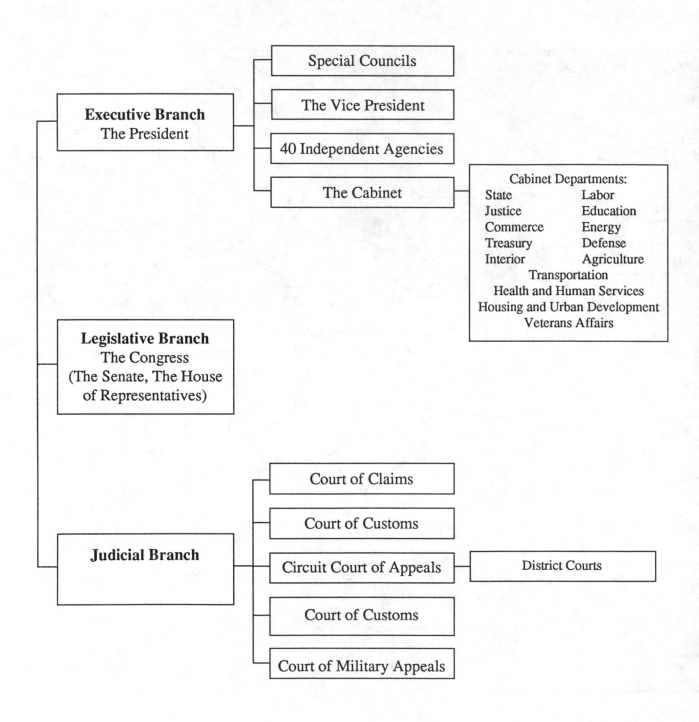

Executive Branch
The President

- Special Councils
- The Vice President
- 40 Independent Agencies
- The Cabinet

Cabinet Departments:

State	Labor
Justice	Education
Commerce	Energy
Treasury	Defense
Interior	Agriculture

Transportation
Health and Human Services
Housing and Urban Development
Veterans Affairs

Legislative Branch
The Congress
(The Senate, The House
of Representatives)

Judicial Branch

- Court of Claims
- Court of Customs
- Circuit Court of Appeals — District Courts
- Court of Customs
- Court of Military Appeals

Appendix 4
Governors and Senators

Alabama
Governor: Donald Siegelman
Term Expires 2002
Senators: Jeff Sessions
        Richard Shelby

Alaska
Governor: Tony Knowles
Term Expires 2002
Senators: Ted Stevens
        Frank Murkowski

Arizona
Governor: Jane D. Hull
Term Expires 2003
Senators: John McCain
        Jon Kyl

Arkansas
Governor: Mike Huckabee
Term Expires 2002
Senators: Blanche L. Lincoln
        Tim Hutchinson

California
Governor: Gray Davis
Term Expires 2003
Senators: Barbara Boxer
        Tim Hutchinson

Colorado
Governor: Bill Owens
Term Expires 2003
Senators: Wayne Allard
        Ben N. Campbell

Connecticut
Governor: John G. Rowland
Term Expires 2002
Senators: Christopher J. Dodd
        Joseph I. Lieberman

Delaware
Governor: Thomas Carper
Term Expires 2001
Senators: William Roth
        Joseph Biden

Florida
Governor: Jeb Bush
Term Expires 2003
Senators: Bob Graham
        Connie Mack

Georgia
Governor: Roy Barnes
Term Expires 2003
Senators: Paul Coverdell
        Max Cleland

Hawaii
Governor: Ben Cayetano
Term Expires 2002
Senators: Daniel K. Inouye
        Daniel K. Akaka

Idaho
Governor: Dirk Kempthorne
Term Expires 2002
Senators: Mike Crapo
        Larry Craig

Illinois
Governor: George Ryan
Term Expires 2003
Senators: Peter Fitzgerald
        Richard Durbin

Indiana
Governor: Frank O' Bannon
Term Expires 2001
Senators: Evan Bayh
        Dan Coats

Iowa
Governor: Tom Vilsack
Term Expires 2003
Senators: Tom Harkin
        Charles Grassley

Kansas
Governor: Bill Graves
Term Expires 2003
Senators: Pat Roberts
        Sam Brownback

Kentucky
Governor: Paul Patton
Term Expires 2000
Senators: Mitch McConnell
        Jim Bunning

Louisiana
Governor: Mike Foster
Term Expires: 2000
Senators: John Breaux
        Mary Landrieu

Maine
Governor: Angus King
Term Expires 2003
Senators: Olympia Snowe
        Susan Collins

Maryland
Governor: Parris N. Glendening
Term Expires 2003
Senators: Paul S. Sarbanes
        Barbara A. Mikulski

Massachusetts
Governor: Paul Cellucci
Term Expires 2003
Senators: Edward Kennedy
        John Kerry

Michigan
Governor: John Engler
Term Expires 2003
Senators: Spencer Abraham
              Carl Levin

Minnesota
Governor: Jesse Ventura
Term Expires 2003
Senators: Rod Grams
              Paul Wellstone

Mississippi
Governor: Kirk Fordice
Term Expires 2000
Senators: Trent Lott
              Thad Cochran

Missouri
Governor: Mel Carnahan
Term Expires 2001
Senators: Christopher "Kit" Bond
              John Ashcroft

Montana
Governor: Marc Racicot
Term Expires 2001
Senators: Conrad Burns
              Max Baucus

Nebraska
Governor: Mike Johanns
Term Expires 2003
Senators: J. Robert Kerrey
              Chuck Hagel

Nevada
Governor: Kenny Guinn
Term Expires 2003
Senators: Harry Reid
              Richard H. Bryan

New Hampshire
Governor: Jeanne Shaheen
Term Expires 2001
Senators: Robert C. Smith
              Judd Gregg

New Jersey
Governor: Christine Todd Whitman
Term Expires 2002
Senators: Robert Torricelli
              Frank Lautenberg

New Mexico
Governor: Gary E. Johnson
Term Expires 2003
Senators: Pete V. Domenici
              Jeff Bingaman

New York
Governor: George Pataki
Term Expires 2003
Senators: Daniel Patrick Moynihan
              Charles E. Schumer

North Carolina
Governor: James B. Hunt, Jr.
Term Expires 2001
Senators: Jesse Helms
              John Edwards

North Dakota
Governor: Edward T. Schafer
Term Expires 2001
Senators: Kent Conrad
              Byron L. Dorgan

Ohio
Governor: Robert Taft
Term Expires 2003
Senators: George Voinovich
              Mike DeWine

Oklahoma
Governor: Frank Keating
Term Expires 2003
Senators: James Inhofe
              Don Nickles

Oregon
Governor: John A. Kitzhaber
Term Expires 2003
Senators: Ron Wyden
              Gordon Smith

Pennsylvania
Governor: Tom Ridge
Term Expires 2003
Senators: Arlen Specter
              Rick Santorum

Rhode Island
Governor: Lincoln Almond
Term Expires 2003
Senators: John Chafee
              Jack Reed

South Carolina
Governor: Jim Hodges
Term Expires 2002
Senators: Strom Thurmond
              Ernest Hollins

South Dakota
Governor: William J. Janklow
Term Expires 2003
Senators: Thomas Daschle
              Tim Johnson

Tennessee
Governor: Don Sundquist
Term Expires 2003
Senators: Bill Frist
              Fred Thompson

Texas
Governor: George W. Bush
Term Expires 2003
Senators: Kay Bailey Hutchison
              Phil Gramm

Utah
Governor: Michael Leavitt
Term Expires 2001
Senators: Orrin G. Hatch
              Robert Bennett

Vermont
Governor: Howard Dean
Term Expires 2002
Senators: Patrick J. Leahy
              Jim M. Jeffords

Virginia
Governor: James S. Gilmore III
Term Expires 2002
Senators: Charles Robb
        John Warner

Washington
Governor: Gary Locke
Term Expires 2001
Senators: Slade Gorton
        Patty Murray

West Virginia
Governor: Cecil Underwood
Term Expires 2001
Senators: Jay Rockefeller
        Robert C. Byrd

Wisconsin
Governor: Tommy G. Thompson
Term Expires 2003
Senators: Herbert H. Kohl
        Russell Feingold

Wyoming
Governor: Jim Geringer
Term Expires 2002
Senators: Craig Thomas
        Michael Enzi

Appendix 5

Structure of State Government

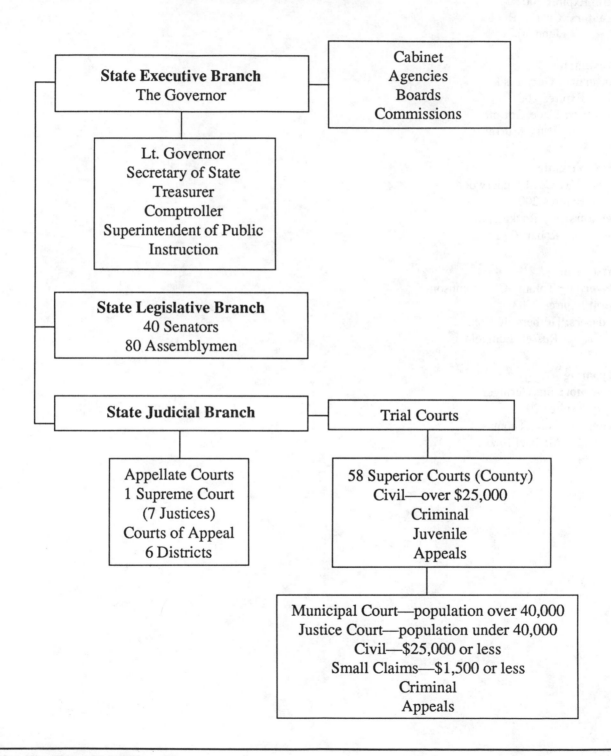

Appendix 6
Summary of U.S. Presidents

PRESIDENT	EVENTS	ADDITIONS
1. George Washington 2 terms 1789-1797 No Party V.P.: John Adams	Commander in Chief in Revolutionary War "Father of Our Country" Constitution established Appointed first cabinet Appointed first Supreme Court	Bill of Rights 11th amendment (States not to be sued in federal courts.) Vermont—14th State Kentucky—15th State Tennessee—16th State
2. John Adams 1 term 1791–1801 Federalist V.P.: Thomas Jefferson	England and France at war American Sailors captured by English Kept U.S. out of English war Alien and Sedition Act Moved into White House	
3. Thomas Jefferson 2 terms 1801–1809 Democratic-Republican V.P. 1st term: Aaron Burr V.P. 2nd term: George Clinton	"Father of Declaration of Independence" Louisiana Purchase Lewis and Clark Expedition	12th amendment (Changed way president and vice president were elected) Ohio—17th state Louisiana Territory paid France $15 million.
4. James Madison 2 terms 1809–1817 Democratic-Republican V.P. 1st term: George Clinton V.P. 2nd term: Eldbridge Gerry	"Father of the Constitution" War of 1812 The Star-Spangled Banner written White House burned	Louisiana—18th state Indiana—19th state
5. James Monroe 2 terms 1817–1825 Democratic-Republican V.P.: Daniel Tompkins	Monroe Doctrine "America for the Americans" Promised protection to 18 newly independent Latin American countries. Missouri Compromise (admit Maine-free, Missouri-slave)	Mississippi—20th state Illinois—21st state Alabama—22nd state Maine—23rd state Missouri—24th state Florida Territory paid Spain $5 million
6. John Quincy Adams 1 term 1825–1829 National-Republican V.P.: John C. Calhoun	Son of John Adams, 2nd president Erie Canal (connected Great Lakes to Atlantic Ocean) Protective Tariffs for U.S. industries.	

PRESIDENT	EVENTS	ADDITIONS
7. Andrew Jackson 2 terms 1829–1837 Democrat V.P. 1st term: John C. Calhoun V.P. 2nd term: Martin Van Buren	"Battle of New Orleans" in War of 1812 Opposed states' rights over federal rights. Defeated National Bank system. Removed Indians to Oklahoma. Texas became independent republic.	Arkansas—25th state Michigan—26th state
8. Martin Van Buren 1 term 1837–1841 Democrat V.P.: Richard M. Johnson	Economic Panic of 1837 Independent Treasury begun	
9. William H. Harrison Term 1 month—1841 Whig V.P.: John Tyler	Served in Revolutionary War and War of 1812. First president to die in office.	
10. John Tyler Remainder of 1 term 1841–1845 Whig No V.P.	First vice president to become president.	Annexed Texas Territory Florida—27th state
11. James K. Polk 1 term 1845–1849 Democrat V.P.: George M. Dallas	Treaty with England for half of Oregon Territory. Mexican-American War Treaty of Guadalupe Hidalgo 1848. Interior Dept. formed	Oregon Territory Texas—28th state Iowa—29th state Wisconsin—30th state Mexican Cession (CA, NM, AZ, UT, NE)
12. Zachary Taylor Term 1 year, 4 months 1849–1850 Whig V.P.: Millard Fillmore	Gold discovered in California. Second president to die in office.	
13. Millard Fillmore Remaining term 2 years, 8 months 1850–1853 Whig No V.P.	Fugitive Slave Law	California—31st state

PRESIDENT	EVENTS	ADDITIONS
14. Franklin Pierce 1 term 1853–1857 Democrat V.P.: William R. King	"Bloody Kansas" pro-slave fight anti-slave groups in Kansas.	Gadsden Purchase paid Mexico $10 million (southern tip of NM and AZ)
15. James Buchanan 1 term 1857–1861 Democrat V.P.: John Breckinridge	"Dred Scott Decision" U.S. Supreme Court upheld Fugitive Slave Law. Secession of six southern states from Union after election. Confederate States of America formed.	Minnesota—32nd state Oregon—33rd state Kansas—34th state
16. Abraham Lincoln 1 term and 1 month of 2nd term 1861–1865 Republican V.P. 1st term: Hannibal Hamlin V.P. 2nd term: Andrew Johnson	Five more southern states leave Union. Civil War "Emancipation Proclamation" First president assassinated.	West Virginia—35th state Nevada—36th state 13th amendment (freed slaves)
17. Andrew Johnson Remaining term 3 years, 11 months 1865–1869 Democrat No V.P.	Reconstruction Act 1868. Set up military government in the south. Impeachment brought against President Johnson Found not guilty.	14th amendment (citizenship to all born in U.S.) Alaska Territory paid Russia $7.2 million Nebraska—37th state
18. Ulysses S. Grant 2 terms 1869–1877 Republican V.P. 1st term: Schuyler Colfax V.P. 2nd term: Henry Wilson	Civil War general Army controlled southern states. Corrupt government "Spoils System" Justice Dept. formed	15th amendment (protects rights of citizens to vote.) Colorado—38th state
19. Rutherford B. Hayes 1 term 1877–1881 Republican V.P.: William A. Wheeler	Introduced Civil Service. Restored dignity and reform to White House. Passed Dawes Act (Indians must homestead land or give it up.)	

RESIDENT	EVENTS	ADDITIONS
20. James A. Garfield Term 6 months, 1881 Republican V.P.: Chester A. Arthur	Tried to support civil service. 2nd president assassinated	
21. Chester A. Arthur Remaining term 3 years, 6 months 1881–1885 Republican No V.P.	Increased civil service. Dedicated Washington Monument. Restrictions on Chinese immigration.	
22. Grover Cleveland 2 term split 1st term 1885–1889 Democrat V.P.: Thomas A. Hendricks	Statue of Liberty given to U.S. by France. American Federation of Labor begun. Apache Indians to reservation.	
23. Benjamin Harrison 1 term 1889–1893 Republican V.P.: Levi P. Morton	Grandson of 9th president Oklahoma Territory opened to settlers.	North Dakota—39th state South Dakota—40th state Montana—41st state Washington—42nd state Idaho—43rd state Wyoming—44th state
24. Grover Cleveland 2nd term 1893–1897 Democrat V.P.: Adlai E. Stevenson	Hawaii became an independent republic in 1994.	Utah—45th state
25. William McKinley 1 term and 1 year, 4 months of 2nd term 1897–1901 Republican V.P. 1st term: Garret A. Hobert V.P. 2nd term: Theodore Roosevelt	Spanish American War with Spain. Cuba independent under U.S. protection. 3rd president assassinated.	Hawaii annexed Spain gave U.S. Guam and Puerto Rico Spain sold Philippines to U.S. for $20 million.
26. Theodore Roosevelt Remaining 2 years, 8 months + 1 term 1901–1909 Republican No V.P. in remaining term V.P. for full term: Charles W. Fairbanks	Famous Rough Rider in Cuba in Spanish American War. Saved natural resources. Established national parks. Commerce Dept. formed. Labor Dept. formed.	Oklahoma—46th state

PRESIDENT	EVENTS	ADDITIONS
27. William H. Taft 1 term 1909–1913 Republican V.P.: James S. Sherman	Sold reserved oil lands. Disagreed with Teddy Roosevelt over use of natural resources. Only president to serve as Chief Justice of Supreme Court. (appointed by 29th president)	16th amendment (federal income tax) 17th amendment (popular election of senators) New Mexico—47th state Arizona—48th state
28. Woodrow Wilson 2 terms 1913–1921 Democrat V.P.: Thomas R. Marshall	World War I Wrote plan for League of Nations. Treaty of Versailles (not ratified by U.S. Senate) Federal Reserve Act	18th amendment (Prohibit making and sale of liquor.) 19th amendment (women's right to vote)
29. Warren G. Harding Term 2 years, 5 months 1921–1923 Republican V.P.: Calvin Coolidge	"Teapot Dome Scandal" Secretary of Interior sold U.S. oil reserve land. First immigration quota. 3rd president to die of natural causes.	
30. Calvin Coolidge Remaining 1 year, 7 months + 1 term 1923–1929 Republican Remaining term no. V.P. V.P. for full term: Charles G. Dawes	"Roaring Twenties" Gangsters and bootlegged liquor. U.S. car manufacturing by Ford, Olds and Buick. Charles Lindberg solo air flight across Atlantic.	
31. Herbert Hoover 1 term 1929–1933 Republican V.P.: Charles Curtis	Stock Market Crash. Great Depression began. National Anthem adopted	20th amendment (changed session of Congress.)
32. Franklin D. Roosevelt 3 terms + 39 days of 4th term 1933–1945 Democrat V.P. 1st term: John Garner V.P. 2nd and 3rd term: Henry Wallace V.P. 4th term: Harry S. Truman	Recovery from Great Depression. Began Social Security system. World War II began. Pearl Harbor bombed. U.S. entered war on Atlantic and Pacific fronts. 4th president to die of natural causes.	21st amendment (canceled 18th amendment.)

PRESIDENT	EVENTS	ADDITIONS
33. Harry S. Truman FDR's remaining 4th term + 1 term 1945–1953 Democrat No V.P. in remaining term V.P. full term: Alben Barkley	World War II ended in Europe. Dropped Atom bomb on Japan. Ended World War II in Pacific. Korean War. Philippines given independence. North Atlantic Treaty Organization	
34. Dwight D. Eisenhower 2 terms 1953–1961 Republican V.P.: Richard M. Nixon	World War II leader. Southeast Asia Treaty Organization. Military advisors sent to Vietnam.	22nd amendment (Limits term of president and vice president.) Alaska—49th state Hawaii—50th state
35. John F. Kennedy Term 2 years, 4 months 1961–1963 Democrat V.P.: Lyndon B. Johnson	Peace Corps formed. First moon landing. Cuban missile crisis "Bay of Pigs" Limited Nuclear Test Ban Treaty 4th president assassinated.	23rd amendment (3 electoral votes for District of Columbia.)
36. Lyndon B. Johnson Remaining 1 year, 2 months + 1 term 1963–1969 Democrat No V.P. remaining term V.P. full term: Herbert Humphrey	Equal Opportunity Commission. Equal Employment Opportunity Act. Voting Rights Act Martin Luther King assassinated. United Farm Workers Organized. Medicare and Medical begun. Vietnam War escalated. Gulf of Tonkin Resolution. 6 Day Israeli War Housing and Urban Development Dept. formed. Transportation Dept. formed.	24th amendment (no tax to vote.) 25th amendment (order for presidential succession and appointing of a president or vice president.)
37. Richard M. Nixon Elected for 2 terms Served 1 term + 5 1/2 months of 2nd term 1969–1974 Republican V.P.: Spiro Agnew (resigned) V.P.: Gerald Ford	Deescalation of Vietnam War. Strategic Arms Limitation Treaty. Visited People's Republic of China. Revenue sharing with states. Vice president Agnew resigned. Congress appointed Gerald Ford as vice president Watergate scandal and investigation. Nixon resigned.	26th amendment (lowered voting age to 18.)

PRESIDENT	EVENTS	ADDITIONS
38. Gerald Ford Remaining term 3 years, 6 1/2 months 1974–1977 Republican V.P.: Nelson Rockefeller (appointed)	First vice president not elected. First president not elected. Pardoned Nixon.	
39. Jimmy Carter 1 term 1977–1981 Democrat V.P.: Walter Mondale	Panama Canal Treaty ends U.S. control in 2000. Camp David Accord (with Israeli and Egyptian leaders) Revolution in Iran. U.S. hostages taken. USSR invaded Afghanistan. U.S. boycotted 1980 Summer Olympics in Moscow. Energy Dept. formed. Iran hostages released.	
40. Ronald Reagan 2 terms 1981–1989 Republican V.P.: George Bush	War in Central America. Appointed first woman to Supreme Court. U.S. Space Shuttle "Challenger" Crashed. U.S. space program badly hurt. Education Dept. formed. Veterans Affairs Dept. formed.	
41. George Bush 1 term 1989–1993 Republican V.P.: Dan Quayle	Berlin Wall came down. Germany United. U.S. troops sent to Panama. Noriega ousted. Break up of eastern communist countries. Hostages in Lebanon. Persian Gulf War - "Desert Storm" Collapse of Soviet Union. Civil war in Bosnia (part of the former Yugoslavia). Starvation in Africa.	27th amendment (compensation of members of Congress)
42. William J. Clinton 2 terms Elected 1992 Reelected 1996 V.P.: Albert Gore	Reinstated President Aristide; democracy restored in Haiti. U.S. peacekeeping troops sent to Bosnia. War in Africa (Zaire, Rwanda, Burundi).	

Appendix 7
Summary of the Bill of Rights

1st   **Freedom of religion.** You can choose what church you want to go to and when you want to go.

       Freedom of speech and freedom of the press. You may say or write what you think is true. Your rights and where someone else's rights begin.

       Freedom to assemble. You can have peaceful meetings and can say you don't like the way things are done.

       Freedom to petition. You may ask the government to make a change or addition to a law or make a new law.

2nd   **Right to have guns.**

3rd   **Right to decide who lives in your home.** Soldiers cannot be put in your home to live unless you give them permission to live there.

4th   **Freedom from unlawful search.** No one may search property without a court order saying they can.

5th   **Right of a grand jury if accused of a major crime.** A person cannot be made to testify against himself. He cannot be brought to court for the same crime twice.

6th   **Right to a fair trial by jury in criminal cases.**

       Right to have a lawyer to defend you.

7th   **Right to a fair trial by jury in most civil cases.**

8th   **Right to fair bails, fines, or punishments.** Bail is the money given to the court to be sure the person will come to court for trial.

9th   **The protection of any rights not named in the Constitution.**

10th **The protection of the powers given to the states.**

Appendix 8
Summary of Amendments 11–27

11th A state may not be sued in a federal court by a citizen of another state or a foreign country. (1795)

12th The president and vice president are to be elected on a separate ballot. (1804)

13th Ended slavery. (1865)

14th Gave citizenship to all born or naturalized in the United States. It also promises due process of the law and equal protection of the law for everyone. (1868)

15th Protected rights of all citizens to vote. (1870)

16th Made federal income tax legal. (1913)

17th Made elections of senators a direct vote of the people. (1913)

18th Made it illegal to make or sell liquor. (1919)

19th Gave women the right to vote. (1920)

20th Change day president took office to January 20 and regular sessions of Congress to January 3. (1933)

21st Canceled the 18th Amendment. (1933)

22nd Limits president's term of office to two terms (or ten years if a vice-president filled only two years of a president's term). (1950)

23rd Gave the District of Columbia the right to vote for president and vice president. (1961)

24th Made it illegal to have to pay a tax in order to vote. (1964)

25th Made the vice president the acting president in case of the president's inability to be in office. It also gives the line of succession to the office of the president and how a new vice president is chosen. (1967)

26th Lowered voting age to 18 years of age. (1971)

27th Compensation of members of Congress. (1992)

Appendix 9

The Star-Spangled Banner

by Francis Scott Key   Adopted by Congress in 1931

Oh, say can you see by the dawn's early light.
What so proudly we hailed at the twilight's last gleaming,
Whose broad stripes and bright stars through the perilous fight
O'er the ramparts we watched were so gallantly streaming?
And the rockets' red glare, the bombs bursting in air,
Gave proof through the night that our flag was still there.
Oh, say does the star-spangled banner yet wave
O'er the land of the free and the home of the brave?

On the shore dimly seen through the mists of the deep,
Where the foe's haughty host in dread silence reposes,
What is that which breeze, o'er the towering steep,
As it fitfully blows, half conceals, half discloses?
Now it catches the gleam of the morning's first beam,
In full glory reflected now shines in the stream.
'Tis the star-spangled banner, oh, long may it wave
O'er the land of the free and the home of the brave!

And where is that band who so vauntingly swore
That the havoc of war and the battle's confusion
A home and a country should leave us no more?
Their blood has washed out their foul footstep's pollution.
No refuge could save the hireling and slave
From the terror of flight or the gloom of the grave,
And the star-spangled banner in triumph doth wave
O'er the land of the free and the home of the brave.

Oh, thus be it ever when freemen shall stand
Between their loved home and the war's desolation!
Blest with vict'ry and peace may the heav'n-rescued land
Praise the power that hath made and preserved us a nation!
Then conquer we must, when our cause it is just,
And this be our motto, "In God is our trust,"
And the star-spangled banner in triumph shall wave
O'er the land of the free and the home of the brave.

Appendix 10
Lincoln's Gettysburg Address

November 19, 1863

Fourscore and seven years ago our fathers brought forth on this continent a new nation, conceived in liberty and dedicated to the proposition that all men are created equal. Now we are engaged in a great civil war, testing whether that nation, or any nation so conceived and so dedicated can long endure. We are met on a great battlefield of that war. We have come to dedicate a portion of that field as a final resting place for those who here gave their lives that that nation might live. It is altogether fitting and proper that we should do this. But in a larger sense we cannot dedicate, we cannot consecrate, we cannot hallow this ground. The brave men, living and dead, who struggled here, have consecrated it, far above our poor power to add or detract. The world will little note, nor long remember, what we say here, but it can never forget what they did here. It is for us, the living, rather to be dedicated here to the unfinished work which they who fought here have thus far so nobly advanced. It is rather for us to be here dedicated to the great task remaining before us, that from these honored dead we take increased devotion to that cause for which they gave the last full measure of devotion; that we here highly resolve that these dead shall not have died in vain, that this nation, under God, shall have a new birth of freedom, and that this government of the people, by the people, and for the people shall not perish from the earth.

Abraham Lincoln, Lincoln Memorial, Washington D.C.

Appendix 11
Glossary

English Spanish

abolished abolió
accomplishments logros
accused acusado
across a través
added agregó
address discurso
afraid temer
against contra
age edad
aliens extranjeros
alive vivo
all over por todo
all the time continuamente
allegiance lealtad
allows permite
although aunque
amend corregir, rectificar
among entre
angry enojado
anthem himno
anxiously ansiosamente
apparently aparentemente
appeal apelar, apelación
applicants solicitantes
appointments nombramientos
approve aprobar
armed forces fuerzas armadas
assassinated asesinado
assistance asistencia
attacks ataques
attempt intento
attended asistió, asistieron
authority autoridad, jurisdiccion
background fondo, trasfondo
basic básicas, básico

be able poder hacer algo
before antes
begins comienza
believed creían
besides además de
better mejor
bill proyecto de ley
birth nacimiento
bloody sangrienta(o)
bloom en flor, florido
bombed bombardeó
brave valiente(s)
bravely valientemente
breaks descanso
bridges puentes
Britain Gran Bretaña
brought trajo, trajeron
brutal bestial, cruel
built construyó, construyeron
built roads construyeron carreteras
business empresa, negocio
businessmen empresarios, negociantes
can get puede(n) obtener
candidate candidato(a)
cannot be no puede ser
care importarle a uno
carry out llevar a cabo
caused causó
cemeteries cementerios
century siglo
certificate certificado
civil civil
claim apropiar
clearance aprobación
climbed escalaron
closed cerro, cerraron

English Spanish

closest más cercano
cloth tela
coal carbón
colors colores
committed cometieron, cometido
complained se quejaban
conflict conflicto
continued continuaban
continuously continuamente
contradict contradecir
controlled controlaba
conventions convenciones
convicted convicto, declarado culpable
correct corregir, corrigiera
cotton gin desmotadora, despepitadora
courage valentía
craftsmen artesanos
created creó
criminal criminal(es)
crops cultivos
dangerous arriesgado
date fecha
dawn amanecer
debt deuda
declared declaró
delivers entrega
demanded exigió
demonstrate demostrar
destroyed destruyó
dictatorship dictadura
died murió
difficult difícil
directs dirige
disagreed no estaban de acuerdo
does business entrar en arreglos
donated contribuyeron
dressed se vistieron

dropped dejaron caer
earned ganó
easier más fácil
easy fácil
Eastern Hemisphere Hemisferio Oriental
either tampoco
emphasized enfatizó
employees empleados
end finales
enemy camps campamento enemigo
enforces hace cumplir
ensure asegurar
entered formó parte
entire todo, entero
establish establecer
events eventos
except excepto
exciting emocionante
exhibits exhibiciones
explorers exploradores
factories fábricas
fail fracasar
farmers agricultores
fear temor
fight back defenderse
fighting lucha
file presentar
files presenta
fill out llenar
fired despidieron
fireworks fuegos artificiales
fishermen pescadores
fleet escuadra de barcos
followers seguidores
forced obligó
forget olvidar(ía)
formed formó
founded fundó

English Spanish

framers redactores
freed liberaron
friendship amistad
furthermore además
future futuro
gave dio
get rich enriquecerse
gift regalo
gives out reparte
go on picnics merendar en el campo
greatly mucho
greet dar la bienvenida
grew cultivar(on)
guarantees garantías
had to pay tenía(n) que pagar
halfway a medio camino
hamburgers hamburguesas
happiness felicidad
harbor puerto
hated odiaba
health salud
Health and Human Services Servicios
    Humanos y de Salud
hearing audiencia
hearts corazones
held celebró
helped ayudaron
highest supremo
holidays días feriados
honor honra
hot dogs perros calientes
housing vivienda
hungry tener hambre
hunters cazadores
hurt lastimar
impeaches denuncia
imports importaciones

improved mejoró
inauguration inauguración
includes incluye
indivisible indivisible, no se divide
inhale inhalar(on)
insure asegurar
introduces presenta
issues asuntos
items artículos
jobs empleos
joined se unieron
justice justicia
juvenile juvenil
kept conservar(on), lograron
kill rechazar
king rey
knowledge conocimiento
later después, más tarde
lawful legal
lawyer abogado
leave salir
left salió
less menos
libraries bibliotecas
light luz
light bulb bombillo(a) eléctrico(a)
lines línea, fila
lint pelusa
lives vidas
loaded cargado
loaned (lent) prestó
losing perder
lost perdieron
loyal fiel
making money ganar dinero
marched marcharon
mass en masa
meal comida

English   Spanish

measures   unidades de medida
miles   millas
minimal   mínimo(a)
moreover   además
mortgages   hipotecas
most   mayor parte
moved   se movía(n)
movement   movimiento
moves   se mueve
murder   asesinato
must live   debe vivir
negotiated   negoció
New World   Nuevo Mundo
no longer   ya no
nominate   nombrar
nominates   nombra
nomination   nombramiento
Northern Hemisphere   Hemisferio Nórdico
notice   aviso
oath   juramento
obey   respetar
obtained   obtuvo
offense   delito
on their way   encaminado(s)
one time   una época
organized   organizó, organizaron
our   nuestro(a)
out of respect   por respeto
over   finalizado, terminado
over and over   repetidamente
own   adueñarse
owners   dueños, propietarios
parades   desfiles
particularly   especialmente
parties   partidos
passage   pasaje, pasadizo
passed   aprobado

permission   permiso
piece   pieza
planned   hicieron planes
plans   planes
play   tocar un instrumento
policy   política o plan de acción
political freedom   libertad política
positive   positivo(a)
potato salad   ensalada de papas
power   poder
print   imprimir
procedure   procedimiento
process   proceso
profit   ganancia
promise   promesa
promised   prometió
protect   proteger
protected   protegía
prove   probar
proven   probado
public charge   carga pública
punished   castigado
purpose   propósito
pursue   seguir
qualified   calificado, calificadas
quietly   silenciosamente
ratify   aprobar
reacted   reaccionar(on)
ready   listo(a)
reasons   razones
rebuild   reconstruir
reexamine   reexaminar
regulate   reglamentar
religious freedom   libertad religiosa
remembered   recordados
remind   recordar
represents   representar
requirements   requisitos

English   Spanish

residency residencia
respected respetado
responsibility responsabilidad
retirement jubilación
returned regresó
rewrite reescribir
right derecho
rivers ríos
room oportunidad
ruled dominaba
runs gobierna
safer más seguro
safety seguridad
same procedure mismo procedimiento
sank hundió
satisfactorily pursuing seguir
    satisfactoriamente
saved salvó
sea mar
security seguridad
seemed parecía
seniority antigüedad
sent envió
separate separado
serious serio
services servicios
share comparte(n)
shares comparte
ships barcos
side costado
sign firmar
signed firmó
simple sencillo
sing canta
single soltero
skilled experimentado(s)
slavery esclavitud

small business empresas pequeñas
sold vendieron
someone alguien
song canción
Southern Hemisphere Hemisferio Meridional
specific específico
speeches discursos
speedy rápido
spokes rayos
spread extendido
square cuadrado, cuadradas
stand ponerse de pie
stars estrellas
started fundaron
states establece
stay out of trouble evitar problemas
stays permanece
step paso
still todavía
Stock Market Crash quiebra de la bolsa de
    valores
stores tiendas, almacenes
strengthen fortalecer
strikes huelgas
stripes franjas
structure estructura
struggle lucha
subdivisions sudivisiones
succeed tener éxito
success éxito
such as tal(es) como
suffered sufrido
sun sol
surface superficie
surrender rendirse
survivors sobrevivientes
swearing-in ceremony ceremonia de
    juramentación

English Spanish

swears jura
taught enseñó
taxes impuestos
tell indicar, decir
territory territorio
thanked dio gracias
Thanksgiving día de acción de gracias
therefore por lo tanto
thought pensó, pensaron
threw tiraron
tired cansaba
tobacco tabaco
torch antorcha
traces indicios
Treasury Dept. Ministerio de Hacienda
treaties tratados, pactos
truth verdad
turkey pavo
understanding comprensión
unhealthy insalubre
unjust injusto
unsafe peligroso, inseguro
until hasta
upward hacia arriba
verdict veredicto
veto veto
violently violentamente
wages salarios
waiver renuncia
walkout paro
war guerra
was called fue llamado
was issued fue emitido
weights unidades de peso
welfare asistencia social
Western Hemisphere Hemisferio Occidental
while mientras

whole entero, todo
will receive recibirá
wind viento
within dentro de
without fuera de
won ganó
worker trabajador
working place lugar de trabajo
worry preocuparse
wrong equivocado incorrecto
yet aun así

Appendix 12
Answer Key

Lesson 1

Activity 1
6
3
1
5
2
4

Activity 2
1. Pacific
2. Canada
3. Mexico
4. Atlantic
5. North America

Activity 3
1. globe, surface map
2. halfway between the North Pole and the South Pole
3. no
4. 4
5. Globes are round and show the whole surface of the earth. Surface maps are flat and can show either the whole world or just part of it.
6. No, there are four.
7. Northern and Western
8. North America

Quiz
1. continents
2. globe
3. Atlantic Ocean
4. south
5. equator
6. oceans
7. continent

Lesson 2

Activity 1
5
4
6
1
2
7
3

Activity 2
Christopher Columbus
Spain
1492
west
tribes
native Americans
North America

Quiz
1. true
2. false
3. false
4. false
5. true
6. true
7. false
8. true

Lesson 3

Activity 1
1. Amerigo Vespucci
2. Spain, France, England, Portugal
3. Spanish explorers
4. Christian religion
5. English and French explorers

Activity 2
explorers
the land
Spain
missionaries
the Christian religion

Quiz
1. b
2. a
3. b
4. c
5. a

Lesson 4

Activity 2
3
6
1
2
5
7
8
9
4

Quiz
1. false
2. true
3. false
4. true
5. true

Lesson 5

Activity 1
3
6
2
9
4
8
7
5
10
1

Activity 2
1. b
2. a
3. b
4. a
5. a

Quiz

1. colonists
2. king of England
3. no
4. yes
5. no
6. colonists
7. climbed onto an English ship and threw tea over the side
8. Boston Tea Party

Lesson 6

Activity 1

1. 1
2. 4
3. 2
4. 3
5. 5
6. 7
7. 6

Activity 2

1. freedom
2. Jefferson
3. birthday
4. Washington
5. Revolutionary War
6. Declaration

Quiz

1. b
2. b
3. a
4. a
5. b

Lesson 7

Activity 1

1. b
2. b
3. b
4. a
5. b
6. b

Activity 2

1. false
2. false
3. true
4. true
5. true

Quiz

1. A document written by the Continental Congress as the basis of a plan of government.
2. 1787
3. Articles of Confederation
4. to revise the Articles of Confederation
5. a. different interests of states
   b. Most people did not want centralized government.

Lesson 8

Activity 2

6
4
2
5
1
3

Activity 3

1. makes
2. enforces
3. explains

Quiz

1. a
2. b
3. b
4. a
5. b
6. b

Lesson 9

Activity 1

1. b
2. a
3. b
4. b
5. b
6. b
7. a
8. b
9. a
10. a

Quiz

1. false
2. false
3. false
4. true
5. false

Lesson 10

Activity 1

1. executive branch
2. native-born
3. four years
4. reelected
5. writes
6. enforces

Quiz

1. b
2. b
3. a
4. a
5. b
6. b

Lesson 11

Activity 1

1. 2
2. 6
3. 4
4. 3
5. 1
6. 5

Activity 2

1. b
2. a
3. a
4. b
5. b
6. a

Quiz

1. the president
2. November
3. Yes
4. Democratic party and Republican party
5. the armed forces

Lesson 12

Activity 1

1. a
2. a
3. a
4. a
5. b
6. b

Activity 3

1. 14
2. secretary
3. State, Treasury, Defense, Justice, Interior, Agriculture, Commerce, Labor, Health and Human Services, Housing and Urban Development, Transportation, Education, Energy, or Veterans Affairs
4. Justice
5. U.S. Postal Service, Small Business Administration, or Commission on Civil Rights

Quiz

1. false
2. true
3. true
4. true
5. false

Lesson 13

Activity 1

wanted
equal power
states
legislature
states
protects
dictators
two
in proportion

Activity 2

4
3
1
2
6
5

Quiz

1. b
2. b
3. b
4. a
5. a

Lesson 14

Activity 1

1. c
2. b
3. b
4. a
5. b

Quiz

4. 6 years
5. to make laws

Lesson 15

Activity 1

7
4
5
2
6
8
3
1

Activity 2

1. false
2. true
3. false
4. true
5. false

Quiz

1. b
2. b
3. a
4. b
5. b

Lesson 16

Activity 1

1. false
2. true
3. true
4. true
5. true

Activity 2

1. Congress
2. yes
3. amend, rewrite, kill, send it to its house
4. House of Representatives
5. He can veto bills.

Activity 3

2
3
5
1
6
4

Quiz

1. a
2. a
3. b
4. a
5. b

Lesson 17

Activity 1

1. local
2. judicial
3. justices
4. explains
5. other
6. final

Activity 3

1. the president
2. Congress
3. for life
4. 9
5. appeal
6. Supreme Court

Quiz

1. false
2. true
3. true
4. true
5. false
6. true
7. true

Lesson 18

Activity 1

1. b
2. a
3. a
4. b
5. b
6. b
7. b

Activity 2

1. true
2. false
3. true
4. true
5. false
6. false
7. true
8. true

Quiz

7
4
5
6
3
1
2
8

Lesson 19

Activity 1

difficult
enemy
Confederate Army
brothers
brothers
against
the issue of slavery
economy
right
Union of the U.S.
Abraham Lincoln

Activity 2

2
1
6
7
8
3
9
5
10
4

Quiz

1. b
2. b
3. a
4. b
5. a

Lesson 20

Activity 2

1. false
2. true
3. true
4. true
5. false
6. false
7. false
8. false

Quiz

2
3
4
5
6
1

Lesson 21

Activity 1

1. England, France, Russia
2. 1917
3. sank American ships
4. 1918
5. Germany and Austria

Activity 2

1. a
2. a
3. a
4. a
5. a

Activity 3

1. a
2. c
3. a
4. a
5. a

Quiz

1. true
2. false
3. true
4. true
5. true

Lesson 22

Activity 1

1. false
2. true
3. true
4. true
5. false

Activity 2

1. The Depression was not in 1829.
2. Factories were not open.
3. Banks were not open.
4. Trade between countries was not easy.
5. The president did not promise money for everyone.
6. Low tariffs did not cause economic problems.

Quiz

1. 1929
2. Franklin D. Roosevelt
3. long lines of people waiting for food
4. Roosevelt's plan to improve the lives of Americans
5. Public Works Administration

Lesson 23

Activity 1

1. Workers started labor unions.
2. There were conflicts between labor and business.
3. Workers were afraid of losing their jobs.
4. Immigrants came from Europe.
5. Immigrants worked for lower wages.
6. Workers faced many problems.
7. Workers worked by the hour or by the piece.
8. Owners cared only about making money.

Activity 2

1. b
2. a
3. a
4. b
5. b

Quiz

1. true
2. true
3. true
4. false
5. true

Lesson 24

Activity 1

1. a
2. b
3. b
4. a
5. b
6. b

Activity 2

3
5
2
6
4
1

Quiz

1. true
2. true
3. false
4. true
5. true
6. false
7. false
8. true

Lesson 25

Activity 1

1. truce
2. Vietnam War
3. January 1973
4. Communism
5. United Nations
6. Lyndon B. Johnson

Activity 2

1. The United States sent troops to defend South Korea.
2. In 1975 South Vietnam was defeated by North Vietnam.
3. The United States sends military troops to help other countries.
4. The United States is a part of the United Nations Security Council.
5. President George Bush sent troops to Saudi Arabia in 1990.
6. Military supplies were sent to El Salvador to help stop the spread of communism.

Quiz

1. true
2. false
3. true
4. true
5. false
6. true

Lesson 26

Activity 1

1. 3
2. 8
3. 6
4. 2
5. 1
6. 7
7. 4
8. 5

Activity 2

1. c
2. a
3. b
4. b
5. a
6. c

Quiz

1. William Jefferson Clinton
2. things outside the U.S.
3. Arkansas
4. things within the U.S.
5. Clinton's vice president

Lesson 27

Activity 1

2
3
4
5
1

Activity 2

1. Christopher Columbus
2. October 12
3. last Thursday in November
4. first Monday in September
5. on federal holidays

Activity 3

1. America celebrates many holidays.
2. Government offices close on federal holidays.
3. Federal employees get a day off on federal holidays
4. Holidays remind us of events in our history.
5. July 4 is Independence Day.
6. Thanksgiving Day is the last Thursday in November.

Quiz

1. true
2. false
3. false
4. false
5. false

Lesson 28

Activity 1

1. red, white, and blue
2. 13
3. stars
4. 7
5. a state
6. Oh say can you see, by the dawn's early light.
7. colonies of the U.S.

Activity 2

1. a
2. a
3. b
4. b
5. a
6. b

Quiz

2
3
4
5
1

Lesson 29

Activity 1

1. The Statue of Liberty was a gift from France.
2. France gave the Statue of Liberty in 1886.
3. The statue is a symbol of a better future to many people.
4. There is a museum on Ellis Island
5. The Statue of Liberty holds a torch.

Activity 2

1. a
2. b
3. b
4. b
5. b

Quiz

1. France
2. Lady Liberty
3. international friendship
4. New York harbor
5. a torch

Lesson 30

Activity 1

1. The Pledge of Allegiance is a promise.
2. Americans pledge allegiance to the flag.
3. The United States is one nation.
4. Liberty and justice are for all.
5. Americans are proud of their form of government.
6. The United States is a republic.
7. In the U.S., government is by the people and for the people.
8. Americans have a democratic form of government.

Activity 2

3
4
5
6
2
1

Quiz

1. true
2. true
3. false
4. false
5. false
6. false

Lesson 31

Activity 2

1. Washington, D.C., is between Maryland and Virginia.
2. Washington, D.C., covers 67 square miles.
3. The Senate and the House meet in the Capitol.
4. The Supreme Court explains laws.
5. The White House is on Pennsylvania Avenue.
6. Washington, D.C., has many monuments.
7. There is a Washington Monument in Washington, D.C.

Activity 3

1. a
2. b
3. b
4. a
5. b

Quiz

1. the president
2. 67 square miles
3. Pennsylvania Avenue
4. Maryland
5. Supreme Court Building

Lesson 32

Activity 1

1. state
2. 50
3. governor
4. constitution
5. Supreme
6. makes
7. cannot
8. cabinet

Activity 2

1. c
2. b
3. c
4. a

Quiz

1. true
2. true
3. false
4. false
5. true

Lesson 33

Activity 1

1. mayor and other elected officers
2. city or municipal government
3. Connecticut and Rhode Island
4. states
5. board of supervisors or commissioners
6. the state
7. city police and city fire department
8. city hall

Activity 2

1. 3
2. 4
3. 2
4. 5
5. 1

Quiz

1. b
2. a
3. a
4. b
5. b

Lesson 34

Activity 1

1. work
2. work permits
3. Social Security card
4. welfare
5. cash
6. public charge
7. benefits

Quiz

1. true
2. true
3. false
4. true
5. false

Lesson 35

Activity 1

1. a
2. b
3. b
4. a
5. b

Activity 2

6
4
5
1
3
2

Activity 3

1. Naturalized citizens can be senators.
2. There is a test for applicants for citizenship.
3. New citizens do swear to be loyal and to defend the U.S.
4. Applicants for citizenship under 50 years old who have not lived in the U.S. for 20 years have to take a literacy test.

Quiz

1. true
2. true
3. false
4. true
5. false

Lesson 36

Activity 1

1. b
2. a
3. a
4. a
5. b

Activity 2

1. obey
2. health
3. citizens
4. government
5. United States

Quiz

1. 4
2. 10
3. 9
4. 6
5. 8
6. 3
7. 1
8. 2
9. 7
10. 5

Appendix 13
Citizenship Spelling Words

Set 1
1. government
2. United States
3. President: Bill Clinton
4. Vice president: Al Gore
5. freedom
6. July 4, 1776
7. Constitution
8. people
9. laws
10. Senator
11. Congress
12. Speaker of the House

Set 2
1. mayor
2. city
3. county/country
4. state
5. tax
6. leader
7. war
8. Sacramento
9. capitol/capital
10. California

Set 3
1. political
2. Democracy
3. Democrat
4. Republican
5. Independence
6. Declaration
7. Bill of Rights
8. Abraham Lincoln
9 amendment
10. judge

Set 4
1. George Washington
2. Christopher Columbus
3. executive branch
4. legislative branch
5. judicial branch
6. American
7. colony
8. pledge
9. flag
10. governor

Appendix 14
Typical INS Video Interview

1. Have you used another name, or an alias, since you came to this country? (An alias is a name that is different from your own.)

2. How do you support yourself?

3. When did you start that job?

4. When were you married?

5. What is the current immigration status of your spouse?

6. Have you ever been involved in any Nazi groups?

7. Have you ever filed income tax?

8. Have you ever claimed to be a U.S. citizen?

9. Do you always tell Immigration the truth?

10. Have you ever knowingly committed a crime?

11. Do you have any traffic violations?

12. Have you ever been arrested?

13. Are you a habitual drunkard?

14. Will you bear arms?

15. Are you prepared to take the full oath of allegiance?

16. Do you belong to any groups, unions, or organizations?

17. Did you fill out this application yourself?

18. Do you want to change your name?

INS officer: "I will make these changes on your application. Sign at the bottom, attesting (agreeing) to these corrections."

Appendix 15
Immigration and Naturalization Service— 100 Typical Questions

1. What are the colors of our flag?
2. How many stars are there in our flag?
3. What color are the stars on our flag?
4. What do the stars on the flag mean?
5. How many stripes are there in the flag?
6. What color are the stripes?
7. What do the stripes on the flag mean?
8. How many states are there in the union?
9. What is the Fourth of July?
10. What is the date of Independence Day?
11. Independence from whom?
12. What country did we fight during the Revolutionary War?
13. Who was the first president of the United States?
14. Who is the president of the United States today?
15. Who is the vice president of the United States today?
16. Who elects the president of the United States?
17. Who becomes president of the United States if the president should die?
18. How many years is the president's term of office?
19. What is the Constitution?
20. Can the Constitution be changed?
21. What do we call a change to the Constitution?
22. How many changes, or amendments, are there to the Constitution?
23. How many branches are there in our government?
24. What are the three branches of our government?
25. What is the legislative branch of our government?
26. Who makes the laws in the United States?
27. What is the Congress?
28. What are the duties of the Congress?
29. Who elects the members of the Congress?
30. How many senators are there in the Congress?
31. Can you name the two senators from your state?

32. How many years is a senator's term of office?

33. How many representatives are there in the Congress?

34. How many years is a representative's term of office?

35. What is the executive branch of our government?

36. What is the judicial branch of our government?

37. What are the duties of the Supreme Court?

38. What is the supreme law of the United States?

39. What is the Bill of Rights?

40. What is the capital of your state?

41. Who is the governor of your state?

42. Who becomes president of the United States if the president and the vice president should die?

43. Who is the chief justice of the Supreme Court?

44. Can you name the 13 original colonies?

45. Who said, "Give me liberty or give me death"?

46. Which countries were our enemies during World War II?

47. Can you name the 49th and 50th states of the Union?

48. How many terms can a president serve?

49. Who was Martin Luther King, Jr.?

50. Who is the head of your local government?

51. Name one of the requirements needed to become president of the United States.

52. Why are there 100 senators in the Senate?

53. Who nominates the Supreme Court justices?

54. How many Supreme Court justices are there?

55. Why did the pilgrims come to America?

56. What is the head executive of state government called?

57. What is the head executive of city government called?

58. What holiday was celebrated for the first time by the American colonists?

59. Who was the main writer of the Declaration of Independence?

60. When was the Declaration of Independence adopted?

61. What is the basic belief expressed in the Declaration of Independence?

62. What is the national anthem of the United States?

63. Who wrote "The Star-Spangled Banner"?

64. Where in the Constitution is freedom of speech guaranteed?

65. What is the minimum voting age in the United States?

66. Who signs bills into law?

67. What is the highest court in the United States?

68. Who was the president of the United States during the Civil War?

69. What did the Emancipation Proclamation do?

70. What special group advises the president?

71. Which president is called "the father of our country"?

72. What Immigration and Naturalization Service form is used to apply to become a naturalized U.S. citizen?

73. Who helped the pilgrims in America?

74. What is the name of the ship that brought the pilgrims to America?

75. What were the 13 original states of the United States called?

76. Name three rights, or freedoms, guaranteed by the Bill of Rights.

77. Who has the power to declare war?

78. What kind of government does the United States have?

79. Which president freed the slaves?

80. In what year was the Constitution written?

81. What are the first 10 amendments to the Constitution called?

82. Where was the Constitution written?

83. Where does Congress meet?

84. Whose rights are guaranteed by the Constitution and the Bill of Rights?

85. What is the introduction to the Constitution called?

86. Name one benefit of being a citizen of the United States.

87. What is the most important right granted to United States citizens?

88. What is the United States capitol?

89. What is the White House?

90. Where is the White House located?

91. What is the name of the president's official home?

92. Name one right guaranteed by the first amendment.

93. Who is the commander in chief of the United States military?

94. Which president was the first commander in chief of the United States military?

95. In what month do we vote for the president?

96. In what month is the new president inaugurated?

97. How many times may a senator be reelected?

98. How many times may a congressman be reelected?

99. What are the two major political parties in the United States today?

100. Why is the president limited to two terms in office?

Appendix 16
INS—Answer Key

1. Red, white, and blue (see page 91)
2. 50 (see page 91)
3. White (see page 91)
4. Each star represents one state of the Union (see page 91)
5. 13 (see page 91)
6. Red and white (see page 91)
7. The stripes represent the 13 original states (see page 91)
8. 50 (see page 91)
9. Independence Day (see page 88)
10. July Fourth (see page 88)
11. England (see page 88)
12. England (see page 23)
13. George Washington (see page 88)
14. Bill Clinton (see page 85)
15. Al Gore (see page 85)
16. The Electoral College (see page 38)
17. Vice president (see page 35)
18. Four years (see page 35)
19. The supreme law of the land (see page 29)
20. Yes (see page 29)
21. Amendments (see page 29)
22. 27 (see page 29)
23. Three (see page 32)
24. Legislative, Executive, and Judicial (see page 32)
25. Congress (see page 32)
26. Congress (see page 32)
27. The Senate and the House of Representatives (see page 32)
28. To make laws (see page 32)
29. The people (see page 32)
30. 100 (see page 47)
31. (Insert local information)
32. Six (see page 47)
33. 435 (see page 44)

34. Two (see page 50)

35. President, vice president, Cabinet secretaries, and heads of federal agencies (see page 35)

36. The Supreme Court and various federal courts (see page 56)

37. To interpret laws (see page 56)

38. The Constitution (see page 29)

39. The first 10 amendments of the Constitution (see page 29)

40. (Insert local information)

41. (Insert local information)

42. The speaker of the House of Representatives (see page 35)

43. William Rehnquist (see page 56)

44. Connecticut, Delaware, Georgia, Maryland, Massachusetts, New Hampshire, New Jersey, New York, North Carolina, Pennsylvania, Rhode Island, South Carolina, and Virginia (see page 17)

45. Patrick Henry (see page 23)

46. Germany, Italy, and Japan (see page 69)

47. Hawaii and Alaska (see page 91)

48. Two (see page 35)

49. A civil rights leader (see page 79)

50. (Insert local information)

51. The president must be a natural-born citizen of the United States; must be at least 35 years old; and must have lived in the U.S. for at least 14 years. (see page 35)

52. There are two from each state. (see page 44)

53. Nominated by the president; appointed with congressional approval (see page 56)

54. Nine (see page 56)

55. For political and religious freedom (see page 17)

56. Governor (see page 103)

57. Mayor (see page 106)

58. Thanksgiving (see page 17)

59. Thomas Jefferson (see page 23)

60. July 4, 1776 (see page 23)

61. That all people are created equal (see page 23)

62. "The Star-Spangled Banner" (see page 91)

63. Francis Scott Key (see page 91)

64. The Bill of Rights (see page 136)

65. 18 (see page 137)

66. The president (see page 38)

67. The Supreme Court (see page 32)

68. Abraham Lincoln (see page 63)

69. Freed the slaves (see page 64)

70. The Cabinet (see page 35)

71. George Washington (see page 129)

72. Form N400, "Application to File Petition for Naturalization" (see page 112)

73. The American Indians, or Native Americans (see page 17)

74. The Mayflower (see page 17)

75. Colonies (see page 17)

76. (1) Freedom of speech, press, religion, peaceable assembly, and to petition for change

    (2) The right to own a gun

    (3) Freedom from unlawful search (see page 136)

77. The Congress (see page 50)

78. Republican (see page 26)

79. Abraham Lincoln (see page 64)

80. 1787 (see page 29)

81. The Bill of Rights (see page 29)

82. Philadelphia (see page 29)

83. In the Capitol, in Washington, D.C. (see page 100)

84. Citizens and noncitizens living in the U.S. (see page 29)

85. The preamble (see page 29)

86. The right to run for public office, to serve on a jury, to hold certain jobs in government offices or with defense contractors, or to obtain a passport and have the protection of the U.S. when traveling outside the United States (see page 116)

87. The right to vote (see page 116)

88. The place where Congress meets (see page 100)

89. The president's official home (see page 100)

90. Washington, D.C. (see page 100)

91. The White House (see page 100)

92. Freedom of speech, press, religion, peaceable assembly, and to petition for change (see page 136)

93. The president (see page 38)

94. George Washington (see page 129)

95. November (see page 38)

96. January (see page 38)

97. The limits differ from state to state (see page 44)

98. The limits differ from state to state (see page 44)

99. Democratic and Republican (see page 38)

100. The two-term limit protects the country from a possible dictatorship. (see page 35)